T0078089

My Youth

Vol. 1

Millard D. Scherzer

authorHOUSE

AuthorHouse™
1663 Liberty Drive
Bloomington, IN 47403
www.authorhouse.com
Phone: 833-262-8899

Published by AuthorHouse 04/22/2022

ISBN: 978-1-6655-5756-6 (sc)
ISBN: 978-1-6655-5755-9 (e)

Library of Congress Control Number: 2022907367

Print information available on the last page.

Thank You To:

Anthony Bielstein, my nephew, for making the suggestion to write my stories that I always tell. Also, Robert Gillaspie for encouraging me to make it a "tell-all" blog about my life.

I dedicate this book to my siblings. William O Scherzer, III, Mary A Fisher, Anna E Bielstein, and Darrell J Scherzer, Sr (post humously). I love them all and my life growth could not have been done without them.

The people and country of India for the huge aceptance and following of my blog, and now, my book, even with a huge devastation over the past years, and today, with the Covid-19 pandemic and a huge countrywide natural disaster. My heart and prayers are with them forever.

My American support and encouragement, including friends and family, in acceptance and prayers throughout this time. Special thanks to Paula Pruitt Rubio, Dennis Butler, Dennis Massey, Leslie Scherzer, Lauretta Heidorn. and more than I can name, for their uncontested and continued support from Day One.

My immediate family and friends for allowing me to include them in stories written as true as I can remember.

The Authorhouse to feel confident enough to publish this book and, hopefully, three more books. One is a children's story. They were involved in the promotion of the book.

Really first, and lastly, to Jesus Christ, my Lord and Savior, who was in my heart and watching over my life during all these stories. Without Christ in my life, the endings to these stories would have turned out much different than they did. I give the glory to Him.

Contents

Preface

My Youth is the beginning of a long spectacular life. It is stories of a naive, poor two year old through his youth to twenty years old. His adventures vary from happy,sad, scary and great. The child was the youngest of five children, seven years apart. Born to a father that was a postal worker at night and a mother that went from secrecretary to nursing to disability. All the while, the children were basically raising themselves. The stories are as true as can be remembered and the lessons learned explain how the boy coped with the changes of the sixties to the eighties. He had to grow up quickly, watching and learning from his older siblings.

Follow ME through the most difficult, yet, special years of MY life. I go from a sexually abused child, to a confused, but happy youth, to a teen confident and ready to show the world that someone can be more than a label that other children assumed.

Everyone Has Something To Give And Many Are Not What Other People Expect. Poor, but smart, I changed my stars and refused to let my past be the reason of my failures, but the source of my successes.

Blog 1: Can a two year old fly?

My adventures start at the age of 2 years old. I know this because we lived on Blossom Lane, Mesquite, Texas in the community of Pleasant Grove. We moved to Seagoville, Texas when I was 3.5 years old in October of 1964. We lived in a two bedroom home with a covered patio converted to a third bedroom. We had a step-down converted garage den. There was only one bathroom. We lived next door to the Pinedas, who were our best friends on the street. Between our homes there was a double chain-linked fence, I can't tell you why. On the left side of the house was white wooden fence that enabled us all to climb onto the roof. We had a multi-colored dog that was named, Sambo.

I tell you these things because they are involved in my stories. It's funny the things we remember when we were young because this was a time of my life that my siblings were so important to me. I wanted so bad to immolate them. I caught on quickly to favoritism, things I should not do and those that I should do. But, I still wanted to impress my siblings as much as I could. In a way, this was a BIG mistake. If they wanted to try something new, it was," Let's get MILLARD....he will do it!!"

So, one day we had a bed and box springs set in the driveway that was in front of the den. My sisters convinced Darrell and me to climb on top of the roof and "parachute" down onto the bed. Darrell agreed that I should go first. The parachute was a sheet with corners tied to both hands and both feet from my backside. Of course I was scared, but they kept assuring me that I was light enough to make it. So, after many minutes of debate and guilty cheers, my sisters got on each side of the bed and said they would count to three, I would jump, then they would catch me. Darrell stood behind me and all three started to count…"one, two (PUSH FROM BEHIND ME)), uhhh, what happened to three?" I found myself hurling to the bed stomach down and arms and legs sprawling. Oh, and screaming my lungs out!

My body bounced onto the bedsprings and then hurled in a flip forward. By the time I could figure what I was doing, I was on my back on top of the hood of the car crying with all my might. So, did I fly? Does it count that Darrell pushed me? I never tried it again, so the answer will never be told! By the way, where was mom or dad? That question will come up many times in my stories.

"What happens when you try to go too far up a tree?"

There were two trees in our yard between the Pinedas. They were next to each other and one was larger than the other. Billy Boy could scurry up both trees with ease. It was not so easy for the rest of us. I had to climb up the fence just to get to the limbs of the smaller tree. After that, I was too scared to go any higher. I was in the house with my mom when suddenly Mary came in from the back informing mom that Anna had fallen from the tree and was stuck between the two fences. We all ran out and I saw Bill in the high tree climbing down and Anna indeed had fallen between the fences. It gets blurry from here but I believe Mr. Pineda and my mother were trying to get Anna out.

Later that evening dad took us children to Mesquite Memorial Hospital to see Anna. Because of our ages, we were not allowed in her room, so we had to look through her room window and wave or write notes to her through it. I remember she had a cast or sling on her arm and also got a stuffed green bunny rabbit that she named Pugsley. Little did I know that at least twenty-five percent of my growing up was going to include hospital visits, usually for seeing my mother one reason or another. When I get to my high school years, my mother's hospital stay will play a very important role about my life.

"How a father gets his 5 young children to take a mandatory shot in their butt."

On one occasion that my mother was hospitalized, the entire family needed to take a mandatory shot to protect us from catching what she had acquired. Dr. Pirrung thought that the best way to do it was to schedule the entire group all at once. So, my dad took us to the clinic, deliberately forgetting to let us know what was in store for us. We all went into the room where the doctor was waiting. We saw the syringes and immediately headed to corners in fear. My dad kept demanding that we each come up to the table and drop our pants to take the shots like brave people. It was suggested that we go in order of age…me wanting oldest to youngest and Billy Boy wanted youngest to oldest. Dad tried bribing the ones who would cooperated. That did not work so he pulled off his belt and threatened to whip us.

When that didn't work, the doctor demanded my dad to be an example and get his first, instead of last. My dad started dancing around saying, ("What? What, what?")! We kids began laughing as he bent across the table and dropped his pants. We moved closer to watch and in went the needle. He was yelping and shaking while saying it wasn't hurting, (even though we all watched tears coming down his face.) I got a little too close and the doctor grabbed me and threw me on the bed pulling my pants down as he carried me. Before I knew it, he had the needle in me and shot me. Though crying, he handed me a lollipop and quickly started chasing another kid as my dad went after another. I sat at his desk while watching the chases around the room. When it was finally over, we all got our suckers while waiting for dad and the doctor to catch their breath. That never happened again……. I wonder why?

"What to do when a tornado is coming down your street."

I was in the den watching television when out of nowhere Billy Boy came down telling us all to get in the closet because a tornado was heading for us. Not really knowing what was happening, I tried to follow his command. It was a very tight fit for us in the closet and Billy kept getting out to look through the window. He finally yelled saying that the tornado was in our front yard. Everyone began screaming, which scared me. I ran from the closet to my parents' room, where dad was sleeping. I slid my body under their mattress and wiggled until I could tell I was below my dad. I flattened my body and waited a good 20 minutes until one of the other kids called my name looking for me. I wiggled my way back out and left my dad's room never waking him up. To this day, I still don't believe there ever was tornado!

………to be continued. Moving to Seagoville, Texas. Ages 4-6 years old. My life forever changed!

Blog 2: Seagoville, Here comes the 2nd Scherzer family

This blog will explain our move to Seagoville, Texas, and a few things that happened when we first moved there in 1964. It will take you from 3.5 years to 6 years old. It will be slightly longer than my first blog for certain reasons. NOTE: The last story might need to be read with an adult. (Hopefully, it will get a child to speak out if you can relate to it.)

"Seagoville, here comes the SECOND family of Scherzers."

Most people did not know that my cousins went to the Seagoville schools a few years ahead of us. Most teachers did, though, because the boys were not known to be prime citizens. We actually moved there because my Uncle was the pastor of Calvary Baptist Church. It was easier to get to my dad's job at the Dallas Terminal Annex. I failed to mention that my mom took us to church as far back as I can remember.

There were less than 1600 people in Seagoville at that time. The part of town where we moved was considered the main community. There were 5 streets that led to the high school. The elementary schools were on the opposite side of town. (Literally around 2-2.5 miles away.) Because we lived so close to the high school, there were no bus pick-ups and we had to walk to school. (Yes, rain or snow, barefoot—not really barefoot, but we could not afford new shoes until our old ones were worn out. Luckily, I was too young for school at that time.

Even though our home was only 1650 square feet, it was a mansion: to me. It had 4 bedrooms, 3 baths, living room, dining room, den, kitchen and two of the bedrooms were masters. Children our ages were living all around us. I was in heaven. I still had three years before I started school, so it did not take too much time for me to get bored. My mom worked the day shift and my father the night. I was by myself until my dad would get home from the bars. Then he just went to sleep. The other kids started getting home around 3:30 pm. I mostly watched children's shows on PBS.

I wandered the neighborhood sometimes, barefoot and shirtless, to find children my age to play with me. I would sometimes go to the store and sell coke bottles to buy candy. Nobody seemed to care that a child of my age was always roaming the neighborhood like this. The first year, Darrell was at home also because he had one year before he started school, too. I was very bored, so Darrell and I got into much trouble for fighting etc.

"The Babysitters"

The first thing to say to the two girls (now in their 60s) is that I am sorry! I hated being left with a babysitter. The minute both our parents were gone, we would hide. I had two very good places: in the dryer and in the linen closet behind the towels. One night, I was so upset, that I never came out of my hiding place and ended up falling asleep. Mom found me around midnight. Needless to say, I could not sit up for a few days after my dad got involved.

At my age 4, Darrell began school. Because my father liked to drink, I was by myself for many days. I learned early in life that you had to fend for yourself. In the 1960s, children were permitted in the beer joints with an adult. Many times dad would come get me, take me back to the bar and while he drank we would play skeet ball, pin ball, darts, and other games. However, the time came that the age limit became 18yo. After that, I easily got passed from neighbor to neighbor while he was out! Little did I know that this would begin a new life for me.

"The games people play."

Again, I thank and apologize to those burdened with me. One day a much older neighbor boy skipped school to "play" with me. I didn't know what he was doing, but I ended up naked and the boy was touching me. Afterwards, he asked me did I liked it and I said "yes". Sometimes, his friend would be there too. This went on for about a year until they moved. They said if I told anyone, I would be beaten up. I never told a soul.

Not long after that, my dad began doing similar things. The only difference was dad would put a pillow on my stomach, so I could not see what he was doing. He too, threatened me, by saying that if I told anyone that he would have to go away and I would never see him again. I loved my dad very much, so I never told anyone. This continued until I was 13 and old enough to say "no"! I will talk more about this later on.

"A swing and a miss!"

One day, my mom was home but I was extremely bored so I decided to call the operator and talk with her. It didn't take long that the operator wanted to speak with my mom. Now, my mom believed in using a switch to spank us while my dad would use his belt. Mom, very angrily told me to go outside and find a switch. Knowing I did something wrong, I searched for a large switch. I brought in a limb from a tree and proclaimed that she might as well beat me since I was so bad. She began laughing and told me just go to my room. (Boy, did I luck out!)

"Learning to read"

At four, my sister Anna taught me how to read. We had the Dr. Seuss series, but I went through them fairly quick. So, Anna had this little book that had larger words. It was about strange animals. I loved reading from it. A good example of it was a poem that said, "There's a crashing bore behind the door! Get a stick and hit it quick!" or "The crafty Lackadazical's talent was magical. Alas, you wouldn't know it because he never cared to show it." You will learn soon that Anna also taught me other things too.

Blog three will be a very important part of my life. Please tell others, and you stay along, too..........

Blog 3: 3-6 years old (con't)

So far I have told a few boring stories, a couple of funny ones, and a couple of very true shortened stories about child molesting. I ask that you keep reading as I grow because things do get funnier, unbelievable, and will make more sense by telling you the earlier ones in the order that they happened. When I get older I will be jumping years that didn't mean much, or even start telling them out of order. I assure that you especially the people that know me, will be blown away. I, also, ask that you try not to leave rude comments. I will be glad to read criticisms. And if you are in any of the situations, I hope that you talk to someone. If you are afraid to talk to family or close friends, I have a private contact page that only I can see the information you send. I WILL respond. If you get bored or curious, just look into my picture gallery it should give you a few laughs. I will keep adding pictures as I go along.

"When a child is looking to be noticed"

There comes a time in every child's life that they want to be noticed above their siblings. The youngest or the eldest are usually the ones that try the hardest. There are 7 years difference between Billy Boy and me. I watched very carefully what the older kids did that got them in trouble or got me praise for something. I put this in my memory because it saved me from whippings later in my childhood. It was a big plus that my closest brother, Darrell, stayed in trouble all the time. This taught me how to keep myself "clean" even when I was the culprit. (I will do a blog just on Darrell and me when I get to my teens. Many funny things will come from that). After I was abused the first few times, I began feeling special. Above that, I began getting a big head because my mom would have me do things like spelling big words, doing math, and give definitions to words to people we ran into. Always hearing how "smart" you are tends to make you believe it. The closer I got to school age, the more I realized that I wanted to learn. And mostly, I wanted to be the best in what I did. All this I credit to my siblings. It wasn't soon before I was considered the smart kid in the family! But the others were the ones who taught me. They just didn't know it.

"Getting lost at the State Fair of Texas"

When I was 5, in 1966, my mom took us kids to the State Fair for the day. Around 10 a.m., we went into the Automobile Building. They always had a children's size car as a drawing and it caught my attention. I let go of my mom and headed over to sign up for the drawing. When I came back, my family was gone! I went around the building MANY times but with no luck. I went out the side door to see if they left the building. I ran directly into a family I knew and immediately explained my predicament. (Now, this family was well known in Seagoville. They went to our church and they knew my family very well.) The father suggested that I go back in to the building and look again. I did, but with no luck.

When I came back outside to tell the family I still was lost, they had disappeared. I was stunned. I thought I had help, but they left me! I began going around the Fair looking through ALL the buildings, searching the Midway, and ending back where I started. Since I was 5, I got into the Fair for free, so I went back to make sure the car was still there. I felt safe as long as the car was still there. Every time that I went through the gate, I talked to the ticket taker. I would make a round about every 20 minutes looking for my family and then returned back to the gate.

Around noon, I was hungry and the man gave me a half sandwich and a shasta to eat and drink. Never once did he tell me to go to lost and found or the police station. I did not know they had one. I went back out to the car, and this time, I got on top of the hood. I fell asleep and when I awoke, it was getting darker. My feet were hurting because of my shoes, so I took my shoes and socks off and placed them on both sides of a tire so if my family left, they would run over them and know that I had been there.

I went back to the gate, but the man was no longer there. I told the new man my situation and he just suggested that I keep going around looking for them.(Darrell and I were both wearing the same shirt. It was a Dallas Cowboy jersey with the same number on them.) The man said that was what people would be looking for to find me. The next round I took, I stopped at Big Tex and sat on the wall there. I figured people would wonder why I was by myself AND bare footed. Still, nothing happened.

I was getting hungry again and back then, the Food Building gave free samples of food to people. I circled the building 3-4 times eating samples until I was full. It was getting very dark and I went back to the gate and checked to see if the car was still there. It was, so I did not panic. Around 8pm, I started to make another round when a motorcycle cop stopped and asked if I had a brother wearing the same shirt. When I said "yes", he put me on the cycle and took me to the police station.

When I saw my mom coming out of the door, I ran to her and finally started crying. I was both very happy and afraid that I was in trouble. My siblings came out and even though we hugged each other, they were very mad at me because mom had not let them do anything all day until I was found. Mom let us ride ONE ride and then we went home. After telling everyone what I did all day, they were more forgiving. On Sunday, at church, my mom had a PRIVATE conversation with the family that I had met. I did not hear her, but her finger was pointing and she did not look happy. I was just glad I was back with my family.

"Going to school"

In our town, we did not have Kindergarten, we had Pre-school. 6 weeks out of the summer, we would go to school for half a day to teach us the "Do's and Don'ts" about being in a classroom. They taught us classroom rules, rules for the bathroom, and how to stay in line in the hallways. I could not wait to begin 1st grade! I did have a problem with having to go to the bathroom many times and I just pretended that it had dried by the time I was to go home. (I learned to control things before second grade.)

Here is something to try to do. Name all your homeroom teachers from 1st-12th grade. For me, they were: 1-Mrs. Mangan, 2-Mrs. Kattner, 3-Mrs. Terguson, 4-Mrs. Miller, 5-Mrs. Morris (Mr. Clopton, Mrs. Welch), 6-Miss Swain (Mrs. Cunningham),(7-8) Mr. Durr, (9-12) Mr. Burch. That's how much school meant to me. It was so funny to me everytime a teacher would ask me if I was the LAST Scherzer. For most of the years my siblings and I would have the same teacher in the designated class at least 2 a year. Darrell left a very high bar for me to reach to prove we were brothers, but not the same. Remember, my cousins went to Seagoville before we did and they assumed we all were like them.

My 3rd and 4th grades were very important in my life, so I will make this Blog short. Get ready for some surprises that even my best friends did not ever know.

Blog 4: 3rd and 4th grade

3rd and 4th grade were very important years for me. I loved my 3rd grade teacher so much. All my family were in Boy Scouts one way or another. My Uncle had left Calvary Baptist Church, so my family switched to First Baptist of Seagoville. So much happened these two years that I could write a book just on them. Since I know everyone really wants the juicy things, then I should be able to keep it to three pages.

Here is where the real good stuff starts. Too bad it did not stop there, also. I will not be giving any names in this part because it affects lots of people. I have prayed and prayed about why I am doing this and I really want it to be helpful to others for hiding things that need to be talked about to someone and to learn that everyone has something in their life you can learn from. So much gets lost in lives because we stereotype instead of learning from different types. This blog will cover the first situation heavily— just warning.

(can you overcome disliking someone)

At the beginning of 3rd grade, I met a boy in my class that for some reason we did not get along together. We were both in cub scouts. We both were considered smart kids. And, at times, we would talk to each other. But, every day or so we would get into a fight after school. We fought, got up, and it was over. That same boy and I crossed paths many times for other reasons all the way to 12ᵗʰ grade. I still do not know what the reason was, we just did not get along.

In 1ˢᵗ grade, my mother started taking classes to become a nurse. I would help her with her tests while she was in school. She became a nurse in my 3ʳᵈ grade and by then I knew I wanted to be in medicine. I learned what many medical terms were by 9 years old. What became clear to me that year, though, was that my mother, also, had many medical "problems". She was going in and out of the hospital for weeks at a time and we kids would have to stay with neighbors, or my paternal grandmother. These two people had verbal fights all my life. (A true Mother-in-law story).

I'm telling these two stories together because the impact they had on me. By the time I turned 9, I had been going to church when I could, usually by bus. One Sunday night I just stepped out of my pew and told the preacher I wanted to be saved. I felt a huge burden lift from me. I went home and told my mother, who was in bed, what I did and she spent about 45 minutes making sure I understood what I did. We prayed together and I went to bed. The next day at school, I went to the boy and apologized for fighting with him and would he forgive me. He did and from that day until now I never fought like that again. (Even though the boy and I never became good friends).

(Are you really baptized if it was under a different name?)

August 9, 1970, I was baptized. I was nervous as it was, not to mention that the water was cold. The preacher reached for me and helped me down into the water. Then it happened! The preacher looked at me and asked me my name.(???) I said, "Millard!"! Then he said, "What?" and a little louder I said, "Millard!" Then out of his mouth he said, "I baptize you, LEONARD SCHERZER......", then he dumped me. People started laughing and I was extremely embarrassed. I always wondered if that really counted since it was not my name, but in my heart I know I'm saved. Things did not change at home when my dad and I were by ourselves. But, two new events happened.

(Meeting a new kid on the street)

I was beginning to do things on my own because I did not think it mattered. I ventured the neighborhood and met new kids. One, in particular, had a weird way of greeting me! He kissed me! We went into his house and his family was not there. You can guess what happened. This went on for a few years when we would get together to play games. You know, preachers and parents will talk and talk and talk about treating a girl respectfully, open her door, etc. But, how many times have you heard them say it was a sin to play with boys.(and vice-versa). I think I can count on one hand!

(Meeting my new family doctor)

My mom's first job as a nurse was at Methodist Hospital in Oak Cliff. She had the second shift which got her home by midnight. Bill was 16 and Mary was 14, so we did not have babysitters anymore. It was hard at times because we had crappy cars that broke down all the time. Bill would come home early from school to take her to work and we all would go at 11pm to get her. We went to Kaufman for medical visits and a new doctor had come in. He needed a nurse so he hired my mother. He was single and very nice to us. He knew our family financial problems and many times he would help.

The doctor lived at Cedar Creek Lake and one weekend he invited us to come for a cookout He had a boat, skis, a tree swing, and many other things to do. We kids were in heaven. The entire second floor was a small long hall full of books and his bedroom. It was a mansion to us. At that point, I really wanted to be a doctor. The doctor did this many times for the next few years and our family and he became very close. Just one problem though, whenever any of us complained of not feeling good, we were taken to work with mom because she would convince us that we might have these horrible sicknesses. This story will continue in following blogs. (This will blow your mind, I sure know it did mine!)

(Running on gasoline)

In 4th grade, I was introduced to sniffing gasoline. (That's what I said, gasoline!) I am not going to explain how it was done because I do not want to give anyone ideas. I will say that when you got high, your whole mind flips out into a kaleidoscope of WOW's. I did this for most of my 4th grade, very naïve to the consequences that I was close to taking. Anytime that I was bored, or just wanted to "escape" for a while, I would sneak to the back yard,(you could not see me because our grass was ALWAYS overgrown), and would partake of the gas. My oldest sister actually caught me one time because we were supposed to be going to Houston and my mom was looking for me. While waiting to go, Mary came out to jump on our trampoline, (the one real good thing our dad bought us). While jumping, she saw me and I came over to her. It was obvious that I was high. She took me to the car and put me in the back seat floor board. This car had a hole in the driver side under the seat and the gas fumes were coming through it. Little did I know, it was keeping me high. Finally, someone covered the hole and turned me around to the passenger side and I slept all the way to Houston. {(WHEW). Nothing was ever said about the ordeal.

(Bill Cosby—the lifesaver)

When we were younger, Bill Cosby would have Saturday morning children's special so often. One in particular time, his special was on drugs and other bad things for children to beware about. He covered all the obvious ones like pot, cigarettes, liquor. But the topic suddenly changed to things that were not so obvious. When he got to the topic of sniffing gas, my stomach sank. Mr. Cosby began explaining the effects and dangers sniffing gas could do to someone and, boy, it got my attention fast. After it was over, I ran to my room and began crying. I thought I did an unforgiveable sin. I finally ran to my mom's room, hopped on the bed, put my head in her lap and busted out, "I'm going to hell and I don't want to!"

It startled my mom and I had to repeat myself. I told her what I had been doing and it took her a very long time to calm me down. She took out the Bible and showed me where God would forgive me if I confessed my sins to him. So, we prayed, mom called the other kids in to explain the dangers and from that day until I was 17, I never touched anything but liquor. And a cigarette that will become another story when I talk about Darrell and me. (It is hard to believe that this was the same Bill Cosby being charged for his own problems, as I write this.) It just proves that no one is perfect and everyone deals with sins daily. As for me, I know God used him to save me that Saturday morning! The one thing I had to remind me of this was an X on my report card for problems in listening. It could have been so much worse.

My next blog will be 5th, 6th, and 7th grade—including the sudden changes including girlfriends, my first brush with the Principal, and new developments in my home front. I promise to include a couple of funny things, too. So stay tuned...........

Blog 5: 5th and 6th grade–
the next layer of my life

"My first girlfriend and Female kiss"

In the summer before my 5th grade, things started to change inside me. The family that lived across the street from us had a girl my age and many times we would play house. She and I were always a couple. We would pretend that we had children and things like that. Well, one day we just got married when I had to go home. She walked with me under the big tree on the street, I took one look at her, then kissed her on the mouth. I told her that that would assure we were still married the next time we played. Then I asked her to be my girlfriend and she said yes! We started holding hands coming from school. It lasted about 3 months.

To many surprises, I had a girlfriend from 5th grade through High School. I just never thought it anyone's business and at school, we were there to learn, not ogle. But, after school and weekend…..In fifth and sixth grade, it was more passing notes between classes, and many dates at the Crest theater on Saturdays, and phone calls.

I remember the year that Central Elementary went to downtown Dallas for a celebration. We did the "Texas Star" square dance in the program. They took us there for about a week of practices, and we sat on the floor with other schools. I met a girl that we flirted between, and after the program, it was close to State Fair Day. I invited her to go with us and she said yes. My dad gave Darrell, my cousin and me one dollar to ride 4 rides. But, the girl had $20. She offered to use it so we could ride many more rides. Though embarrassed of the situation, we had a great day.

When we took her home, she invited me to a Halloween party at her house. My parents allowed me to go and we went as Raggedy Ann and Andy. We won the prize for best couple costumes and I got a candle shaped like a skeleton head. When you lit it the wax would come out red like blood. It was cool because when the wax burned down to the eyes, ears, nose and mouth, the bloody wax would drip out of them. I thought it was real cool. We broke up soon after, as kids do, and I found other girls to write letters.

In 6th grade, a new girl came to my class. I had never seen her, but I knew we would be friends immediately. I found out that her sister was becoming best friends with my sisters, and so we got closer and closer as friends. That friendship is still there today, unless this blog changes it. She will be in many of my stories to come.

(What you do when you do not have lunch money)

Every week, dad would usually put EXACTLY the amount for a lunch tray (Nothing extra). But many weeks, the money would not be there. I learned 2 magic card tricks that during play period, I would perform them until I had enough money for lunch. I, also, was not shy to ask someone for something off their plate if they were not going to eat it. I truly never knew if we would have dinner that night or not, so I ate what I could at lunch. You might say lunch was always "Magically Delicious"!

Blog 6: National Boy Scout Jamboree

The summer before 7th Grade, I had been in Boy Scouts just over a year. Our troop planned to go to the National Jamboree in Idaho. It was going to be one week driving up, a week at the Jamboree, and a week coming home. For all of us to go would cost $4000. My father said he absolutely would not pay the way for my brother, Darrell, and me. So, for us to go we had to participate in MANY fund raisers.

I wanted to go to the Jamboree very much. So, I participated in every fund raiser that came along. The money would be split between all the scouts that participated that day. We sold everything from fireworks to light bulbs. It didn't take me long to get mine paid. (I learned very quickly how to accept "NO" until you get the one "YES".) The firework stand was the easiest. People came to us. Our goal was to get them to buy more than they came for! We slept in tents and a camper, rotating who got the camper.

However, Darrell was not as eager to work so hard, so he was still behind on his quota. It sounds cheeky, but I started participating to pay his way. (I will be designating an entire blog about Darrell and my relationship. I promise you will love it.) Once we reached our goal, we were on our way. The trip was, in easy words, the best and worst thing to happen. The escapades about 16 teenage boys with only 2 adults can be rather cumbersome. Camping all the way. We had our good days and we had our "hellraiser" days.

On the drive, to and from, we saw many sights. The Old Faithful Geyser was the best, but going through the mountains came in a close second. After the first week, the leaders took us to this town to restock on groceries, as guys went around town looking for a laundry mat,(and girls to talk to!) We were going down a street with our laundry in backpacks. Suddenly, we saw these two girls come out of a building and like heathens, we yelled and began running towards them. The girls screamed and ran back into the building. To our luck, it was a laundry mat!!

Even though we were in scout uniforms, the girls kept screaming as we came inside. We apologized and showed them our clothes to prove we were not there to bother them. After calming things down, the girls began talking to us. They both were seniors, I was 12. Because of my age and size, I guess I was not too much of a threat so one of them sat on a table and talked to me. Her name was Rosebud. When they were ready to leave, she gave me her name and address and we became pen pals for about 2 years.

After Rosebud graduated, she got married and, of course, her last name changed. Not long after, she got pregnant and we wrote through her pregnancy. But, when the baby came, Rosebud told me we would have to stop writing because of her new life. I actually wrote her a poem titled "Rosebud" and sent it to her thanking her for her friendship. She sent me a picture and the writing stopped.

(Oh, yea, the Jamboree.)

The Jamboree was awesome. There were scouts from all over the globe. It was huge and so much to do if you like the outdoors. We got to meet the REAL Colonel Sanders when he furnished a supper one night. Better than that, we had Bob Hope do a stand-up show. A few of us guys were walking through the trails when we heard what sounded like a microphone. We followed the sound and ended at an open hillside where people were setting up a stage. We were afraid to get too close so they would not tell us to leave.

As we sat on the hill watching and listening, all of a sudden Bob Hope came out on the stage. We could not believe it. We slowly kept scooting down the hill to get a better look, but kept our distance. Mr. Hope began testing the microphone while rehearsing his act. He looked up at us and said "You boys wave if you can hear me from there!" Stunned, we wave and he said "do I sound alright?". We waved again. They let us stay while he continued rehearsing, then he left the stage. Though we were too scared to go up to the stage and get his autograph, we ran back to camp and told everyone what happened. We told them a joke he told, but they did not believe us. That night, after he told the joke, everyone was looking at us and we just smiled from ear to ear.

The joke went like this, "A grasshopper hopped into this pub and jumped onto the bar. The bartender came to him and said {"You know, we make a drink named after you!"} and the grasshopper replied, {"you make a drink called IRVING?"}…. Oh, come on, he was performing to kids. Did you really think it would be dirty? …I will continue the Jamboree in my next blog. My fingers are getting sore and I have so much more to tell.

Addendum and Clarification (WARN)

Before I finish the story of the Jamboree, I want to clarify and warn that my story is not intended to be over PG, but, there will be parts that readers might not want to read, but maybe should. I am not justifying my life decisions to make me look like a victim and everyone else predators. I simply want to tell the truth. I need to jump back a little. During my last few blogs, I deliberately left out the obvious. That is, I still had my male friends that liked having experiments. It was simple since we were taught to respect girls.

Before I can tell the next story, I need to add that during that same spring and summer, my mom's boss took a liking to me. Whenever my mom took me to see the doctor, he would have her put me in his private office. Thinking he was just doing exams on me, I learned later there was another reason. He began asking my mom to let me spend the weekend with him to do yard work, etc, and he would pay me. I wanted the money, so I said yes. Again, without getting crude, the first visit made it quite clear why he wanted me there. All I will say is that like my dad, it was more than experimenting. But, I allowed it. I began thinking I must be special to these people, if it was ME that it happened. (Readers, please teach your children that this is a ploy! They want you to feel special, when it's all lies. If it was not me it was someone else in the same situation!)

However, at the end of the weekend, I would get paid much more than just for mowing a lawn. That I REALLY liked. This happened during a year and a half. I will have one more story about the doctor, but after I tell some fun stories about my brother and I, and this next story.) Read it without condemnation but reality and understanding of my decisions. No excuses, but coming from a poor family and never having money. (I do not regret my past.) I consider myself a survivalist, determined to show my mistakes, as well as my determinations. So, on to Blog 7..........

Blog 7: Continuing the National Boy Scout Jamboree

(What I would not do for the money).

One day at the Jamboree, I went by the Commissary,(general store). I found these bracelets that one said "Mother" on it and 2 said "Sister" on them. The total was going to be $5 for all three. My dad had only given me $10 to last 3 weeks. I went back to camp and ask Darrell if he still had any money and he did not. My (then) brother in law and his brother could not help me either. So, I started asking other scouts if I could borrow the money for them. They all said no, but one boy. He said he would give me the money if I would do one thing. He wanted me to stay in their tent that night and allow them all to do whatever they wanted to do to me. I was shocked!

I really wanted the gifts for my mom and sisters. There were two respectable boys that I looked up to that told me to do it. They assured me nothing would probably happen. So, I told them yes. That night, I got in their tent and just laid there. However, the guys started touching me and doing things that young boys sometimes did. The irony of it was that I did absolutely nothing but lay there. For about 10-15 minutes, the other guys took turns "playing". Then everyone went to sleep. I got the money and bought the items thinking nothing great of the night.

To my surprise, when we started 7th grade, for about a month, a rumor got passed around that I would do anything for money. It was being told by one of the boys who participated that night. I wanted to blow his cover so bad, but I knew it would just make things worse. I just ignored them. THEY were the ones doing something, I just laid there. I felt very dirty and ashamed, though. When I got older, I realized that I prostituted my body to them, which made me no better than them. Finally it stopped and things went back to MY norm. I even got nominated (and won) that year to be the Junior High Student Counsel President.

Each year, I tried to be the best in everything I did. I have a big head and thought I was the greatest in everything I did. Back then, everyone played to win, You got awards for 1st, 2nd, and 3rd and all got a certificate of participation.

(Lat day of Jamboree)

On the final day of the Jamboree, We had a talent show. We auditioned to be chosen as one of the acts, We won the right to sing last and close out the ceremony. We sang, "The Night they Drove Ol' Dixie Down" I fell in love with music and singing when I was smaller. We got a standing ovation. It was great. That was probably the best part of the Jamboree. When we finally got home, there was so much to tell. I cannot think of a better way to leave than after that night's banter.

Blog 8: Another crossroad

I got permission to use my friend's name. The girl I met in 6th Grade was Terri. She became my best friend forever, but not without things that happened. I really, really liked her. We had a lot in common. We both had good grades, loved camping, and during the free time that I had in the summer, we spent a good portion of it riding bicycles, and learning how to do competitive swimming, But, we learned to finger spell so we could talk without others knowing it.

Both Terri and my older siblings were doing the same, as becoming very good friends. We would ride our bikes on top of the school. If the swim team or Explorers did something that required a date, we just automatically grouped up so we could come as well. With Terri and I, it was a convenient relationship. But, I felt feelings for her that were ONLY for her. I knew that they would never be acted on since I had her on such a high pedestal. Terri was and still is a special person to me. Both of us knew that it was a given to help each other when things got desperate. No questioned ever asked. I thank her very specially.

(Was I kidnapped during my 7th grade?)

One morning, my dad came home very distraught. He drove my sister's convertible car, because it was the only one working at the time. He said that near Bexar Street on Highway 175 that he had be robbed. After pleading very hard, we could not convince him to call the police. He said they stole my sister's "letter" jacket, his wallet, cash, etc. but he was afraid they would do it again, if he told the police. I assumed he forgot that I was always at home by myself.

That Tuesday, my mom and the other kids went to the Explorer's weekly meeting. My dad left about the same time to go to work, leaving me alone, as usual. I was afraid that the thief would return since he had our address. So, I took about 10 aspirins and convinced myself to runaway from home. By the time I reached the highway, I was picked up. (Yes, I know who it was, but it will go to my grave.) They let me off at Kmart on I-30 and Buckner.

It was getting dark and colder, so I gave up and decided to tell someone I was kidnapped and to call the police and call my mom where she was at! When the police arrived, I never described the car or the person correctly to protect him, but the police saw right through that quickly. At this point, I just wanted to get dad to report the robbery. I began crying on the way home and told the police it was for that reason only that I did this debacle. There was a large crowd at my house so I stayed in their car until mom and dad came to get me.

Instead, they got in the car with me and while I was giving my statement, dad was giving his own. I was relieved until school the next day and it was all anyone was talking about. This is the first time I am telling the truth about what really happened.

(Little Anthony, at that time called Del, short for his middle name.)

During the last part of my 7th grade, Anna announced that she was pregnant and that she would be getting married to Del's father. I was excited and she had Del the summer before my 8th grade, Anna's marriage was short lived. After the divorce, I was designated as Del's babysitter. This changed my life completely. Anna had to get a job to support Del, and besides swimming and scouting, I had nothing else to do. I felt like a father, so I started teaching Del all I could. This went on for 4 years.

(Going back to my doctor story for a moment.)

One Friday morning, before Del was born, My mom woke me up and told me to get dressed and pack for the weekend because the doctor needed me to help him. I tried to refuse…. I used every reason I could not to go, but finally mom reminded me that this was her boss and her job depended on me going! That's all she had to say to give me guilt enough to go. I could not tell her the real reason, and I did need money! I have no reason to say what happened, because I have told you before. A few months later, mom asked me, in front of dad, if the doctor ever did anything to me. Of course, I said no. She proceeded to say that 3 other families went to court about his escapades and he was sent to jail. What a relief! I did not ever admit it to mom, but I felt she already knew. Mom lost her job, and suddenly started becoming sick to everything and it was affecting her heart. (that is another story.)

Blog 9 will finish 7th grade and 8th grade….. after that I promise to use Blog 10 to tell about Darrell and my relationship. I have 5 VERY funny stories to tell about us. Stay with me and stay tuned…..Thanks!

Blog 9: Babysitter, Self-proclaimed Know-It-All, and more

(Self Proclaimed Know-It-All)

By the middle of the seventh grade, it was pointed out by my mom that I had never made a grade lower than an A on any report card. She would tell everyone this, which got me believing that I was special. It was around the time that "cliques" began and I was "placed" in the smart group. I loved school, and I loved to learn. Because I still hung around the guys, (girls were our enemies!), I ran for Jr High Student Counsel President. We had a pact between other guys running, that all the guys would vote for the guys running. I won and thought I made the popular group. The hardest part was that Terri ran for President, also. I did not know this until we made our first announcements. I did not want to compete against her because I already knew what the guys were doing. But, I DID want to run! Later that year, they had the Cheerleader tryouts. I signed up to run to be the Mascot. Terri signed up for cheerleader. Boy, the rumors flew, but I did not care, until the unthinkable happened. A student broke her leg and was unable to tryout. The sponsor made her the MASCOT! I had to tryout for cheerleader, which I DID NOT want. No other guy ran because it was a "girls" club. To say the least, I blew it badly. But, I prayed very hard for Terri and she won. This made me feel exonerated for winning President. Our friendship stayed strong.

One night, Billy Boy and I took dad to work. In downtown, there was theater that had the word, "Homosexual" on it. Billy started saying how sick and perverted it was. I did not understand. I asked DAD what it meant and he told me saying the bible called it a sin. I fell into my seat and got very quiet. I kept saying it over and over and over in my mind," I am a homosexual, I am a homosexual!" I did ask what do they call a regular boy/girl relation and they told me. Then I asked about someone who liked both. They said it was "bisexual.".…. Okay, I could live with that! I still wanted to pretend that I was straight. To do that, I had to have multiple identities. At school, because of my grades, I was placed in classes that might have 5-6 guys and the rest were girls. Out of school, I had to have true boy FRIENDS. (to make this easy, if you saw me walking around school or around town with another guy, they, to my knowledge, were straight. My third thing was to hide anything about a guy that I liked or had hooked up with. I just hoped that they did the same. Their secrets were AND are safe with me.

I really liked girls. In seventh grade, another elementary school came to our Jr and High school. This very nice, smart and cute girl with long hair sat in front of me in a few classes. I acted like a fool, just like many other 7th grade boys. I had a way of taking my pencils and braided her hair without her feeling me do it. I left the pencils in her hair to keep the braids in place. Many times, she walked out of the room unknowing what she looked like. I thought this would get her to like me. (HELLO!!!!!) I did it in 8th grade, too. But as I got to know her, I wanted to be her friend. We are to this day! We helped each other with our homework, and realized she was straight A's, as well. The girl invited me to go to her church. I said yes, and again, I got active in church and tried to do things biblical. But, during this time, things at home were still changing at a blink of an eye.

My maternal grandmother died. Within months, my grandfather remarried. At the same time, my step-aunt moved in with us. Anna found out she was pregnant while I was still 12. She and her then boyfriend got married. I turned thirteen in March and they had Del that summer. My family was very active with scouting and my mom was beginning to have "allergies" to the world. They thought it was affecting her heart so she was in the hospital many times that year. Terri and I still had our special friendship and we both started practicing on the swim team after school. My sister had to work when she divorced and I had to take care of Del when she did. I loved Del as if he was my own. I taught him all I could, and took him to church with me when I was allowed. But, my Aunt made a deal with me in eighth grade. Since she was very active with her boyfriends, I was the only one to care for Del. So she taught me how to drive, if I would pick up her boyfriend, go to the store, then drive around so that they could spend time together. I stipulated that she had to get me a large bag of M&M's. Later, she showed me how she got the candy, and other things, by stealing them. This was before stores had cameras. It worked every time. I could not get myself to do it though.

One day, it was my dad, Del and I by ourselves. I was confronted about doing something with dad. I looked down at Del in my arms and pictured something like this happening to him one day. I took a deep breath and told my dad no. I said it was over and if he tried to do anything like that to Del, he would regret it for the rest of his life. He never touched me again and stayed away from Del. He knew I meant it, and as far as I know, nothing ever happened to Del either.

(Being Student Counsel President)

I wanted to be friends with everyone. I always felt bad when people would pick on other kids just because they were different. If that happened, I made it my desire to meet the person and become friends with them. As for President, I was more selfish than really helpful. My goal was two things. One, to get the National Jr High Honor Society placed in our school. (Why? I knew I would be selected to be on it.) Second, I pushed to have a Jr High Homecoming and include choosing a Homecoming Princess! {Why?) I got to crown the Princess, and I kissed her on her cheek. They both passed and everything went my way. Two other things happened in eighth grade. Terri and I learned finger spelling and could help each other on tests without anyone knowing. Of course, we knew most the answers, so it was just a way to assure we got an A. Second,(very unbelievable) another A student and I had Earth Science together and we sat next to each other. The teacher gave a VERY HARD test one day and we helped each other a lot. The next day, the teacher did not pass back the tests. When asked why, he said, "If my two best students had to cheat to pass, it was too hard of a test, So I threw it away!"

I learned a big lesson that day. Teachers had to meet a quota of A and B students each year to keep their job. We were already chosen to be the A students. I learned that we could get away with murder. And we did. I promised that Blog 10 would be about Darrell and me. So, I will begin 9th and 10th grade in Blog 11. More surprises start there. I hope you really enjoy Blog 10....

Blog 10: Tribute to my Brother, Darrell

Finally…..we get to talk about my brother, Darrell. Darrell was two years older than me, and because of that, we had to share a room most of our childhood. He was my closest friend and my worst enemy. He past away at age 47. We had not been able to be together for a few years before that with the exception of the summer before he died. Darrell, his wife, and their youngest son made a trip to see me while I lived in North Carolina.

That summer, we rented an apartment on the coast, and had a terrific visit for a week. It was their anniversary and we went all around the coast including going around Wilmington, Cape Fear, took a ferry boat to see the Aquarium, and just have a blast at the beach. Les, his wife, is like my real sister, and I enjoyed my nephew. (He got soooo sunburned!) If I am correct, they always went to Golden Coral for their Anniversary and we found one on our way back from Wilmington. It was perfect. I thank God that they came because that was the last time I saw Darrell. It thrilled me that we parted ways with that visit. It is my fondest memory of him. These stories are in celebration (though they may not sound like it) of his life with me. They will not be in any special order.

For people that thought Darrell was not a bright person because he made bad grades, always got into trouble, was over-weight, and he had a hard time making friends, let me tell you that Darrell was the smarter between the two of us when it came to IQ tests. Twice out of three times, he surpassed 140 points which was considered a genius. He made bad grades and did stupid things in class because he was bored. They would not advance him because of the grades, but they should have done so. I was jealous because my highest IQ was 133. My lowest was 124.

(When it rains….it pours!)

Darrell had a bed wetting problem, like many people, for many years. We had to share a bed. I hated it. There I was, having a great sleep when all of a sudden I would wake with this warm, wet feeling up and down my body. I would jump out of bed and wake him to go to the bathroom. We would have a set of sheets waiting by the bedside for such an occasion. It would not have been so bad except Darrell slept "au natural". I learned to sleep at the edge of the bed and to this day, I cannot sleep in the middle of a bed. He sweated, too. It would drive me crazy if he turned and touched me. For a few years, we had our own bed. then we had the tape across the floor with, "This is MY side, That is YOUR side' which most siblings went through at one time or another.

(A stitch in time….means 9, stitches that is.)

It was no secret that our home was probably the filthiest in Seagoville. With my parents hardly ever around to enforce things, our bedroom was hideous. My dad had from Saturday morning until Monday evening off every week. So if he came home drunk and in a foul mood on Saturday, it was chaos for us. One such weekend had Darrell and I stuck in our room until it was spotless. As always, we played around, as well as, cleaned.

During a scuffle, I dropped a glass and it broke on the floor. For the time being, I swept it up and placed it into a shoe box top. About that time I was called to the phone to take a call. Darrell got mad at me for taking so long so he came into the kitchen and hung up the receiver. I got so angry that I took the phone handle and bopped him across the head fairly hard. (BAD MISTAKE and I knew it.) I dropped the phone and started running from him. I ran into our room and tried to make a dive across the bed. But, I had left the lid with glass on the floor. My left foot landed directly into the middle of the box! When I pulled it out, there was a huge piece of glass lodged in my foot. I pulled it out and it was so deep, I saw the inside of my foot before it started bleeding. My dad had to rush me to the Emergency room in Kaufman where they placed 10 stitches inside the cut and 9 outside. I was on crutches for three weeks. Darrell and I both still got the wrath of my dad when we got home.

(I need some air, someone open a window!)

One day the family was playing cards at the dining room table. There were not enough chairs, so I stood at the end of the table in front of a floor to ceiling window. I could not stay still, so I was using my hands to rock back and forth on the table. I said something about Darrell losing, or similar. He timed it just right to THUMP his end of the table so that my hands slipped. You guessed it, I missed grabbing the table and next thing I knew, I had fallen THROUGH the window. Luckily, I was not hurt. This was one of those times that, after dad got hold of him, Darrell hurt worse than I did.

(There are different ways to score in Darts.)

Darrell and I were playing darts and I was winning. After one of my turns I was gathering my darts from the board. When I turned around, Darrell was in the process of throwing a dart at me. He hit me in my forehead right between my eyes. The dart stuck there just hanging. I went running to my dad while Darrell was begging me to yank the dart from my head. I refused and kept telling him "This is my proof!" Of course he got in huge trouble from dad!

(The spoon Tattoo)

On another occasion, whatever I did to make Darrell mad, he chased me around the dining table. He kept yelling, "stay still!", but I kept going around. Finally, he picked up a spoon and with full force, he threw it hitting perfectly on my right upper arm making a whelp of a spoon. No one was home at the time. So, i took a pen and traced the whelp into a perfect spoon. I left it there until I could tell on him and I had the proof to show. (having proof was my best ammo.)

(Did he really do it?)

Now, I was not the victim all the time, but since Darrell always stayed in trouble, mom and dad believed me. I did many shameful things. I would tell Darrell to just wait. When my chance came, I would hit MYSELF in the chest or slap my face leaving finger marks,(remember, for the proof.), and run crying to my parent saying Darrell did it. The other way to get him in trouble was to say that Darrell took dad's gun and pointed it at me! That was always the best one. When we got old enough, all of us were in the living room confessing about things we got away with doing. When I confessed that I lied many times to get Darrell in trouble, my dad began to weep,(because he BEAT, not just spanked, when he was angry.) He apologized to Darrell, then took him out to eat.

(Justice gets its reward, kind of)

Finally, one day I was babysitting Del, but I was in my bedroom while Darrell and Del were in the den watching TV. Del came screaming into my room and jumped behind me on my bed. Darrell followed with a belt in his hands telling Del he was going to beat him.(it was something stupid). I blocked his swing and his belt hit me. (Darrell was twice my size and if he got a hold of me, I was a GONER). I lifted my legs and was able to kick Darrell into the hall and get Del underneath me. To protect Del, I had to just lie there over him allowing Darrell the ability to beat the devil out of me. It was the worst beating Darrell ever did to me, as well as his last. But, he never got to Del!

I could go on and on about Darrell. Even though they were mean stories, we had our times that we protected each other and had great fun. They just are not as fun to tell in stories. I Love and Miss him very much.

Blog 11: 9th grade

My goal was to be the best in everything. I was very competitive in all I did. That was how I got my attention. I was very materialistic, too. I have 27 trophies. 19 medals (9 gold, 7 silver and 3 bronze—and a bronze medal for National coed volleyball), and way too many ribbons and certificates. They were mostly for swimming, but they include tennis, baseball, football, pool, bowling, and volleyball. I am telling this now because this was the time period that I won many of them. Now, they are just items and only mean something to me.

(Surprise on the swim team)

Terri and I won Rookies of the year our 8th grade in swimming. We decided to keep swimming during the summer and both became much faster because of it. When school started, the swimmers were placed in the lane for practice that had people they were most equal to in time. Two fastest lanes were in the middle two. It was a huge surprise when I was placed in the fastest boys lane with three juniors. I was not liked at first, but eventually we all became a team and we had no problems.

Terri and I became the first 9th graders to Letter. I lettered every year of high school.

I know this is bragging, but it was something I did and it was special to me. I stayed in scouting and at 15 I joined the Explorers. The summer between 8th and 9th grade was the first year I became a lifeguard at the (now gone) city pool. I loved that job and it was great having my own money, (even if it was just for the summer.) During this time, I did not have to beg to my dad for cash. Mom became very active with the Explorer post and began going into the hospital more often.

You need to know that when my sisters were in high school, they had many parties at my house and Terri and I were able to sneak our way into them. At that time, kids could drink alcohol if we had a guardian. My parents agreed to be the guardians as long as everyone brought a permission slip from their parents to drink. (Yeah, right. Most letters were written and signed by the participants.) I would always sneak drinks that people sat down. I got drunk many times. *As I said before, it was no secret that my family lived in filth. It took a lot, (usually with help from friends) to clean the house well enough for dad to let us have the parties.*

(Living in private shame)

One time, dad came home very drunk. He was in a horrible mood, Being Saturday, most of us were still in bed asleep. Dad came to each of our rooms with his belt and demanded we come to the living room. When we got in there, dad went through each room and kicked and pushed everything, (even just shoving things off the dining room table). He made a huge pile and he had us get in it, He told us we could not leave the room until the pile was gone, It took all day, and then we had to do laundry, dishes and bathrooms. You would think we would have learned a lesson, but before long, the entire house was back as it was before. We had roaches, mice, and even rats.

As far as my life, I had a girlfriend almost the entire year all during high school. We had an understanding that at school, we showed no affection. I was afraid of anything being said. But, outside of school was a different thing. My girlfriends were all involved in either swimming, scouts or both. We spent many hours together and I put them all on a pedestal. I tried to do what the Bible taught us to do, but that did not stop other things from happening. I never had to do anything, they just happened. When someone, (many nice looking), made advances, I did not turn them down. We were taught in church to respect women, but very few talked about any other actions. And besides, It was all I knew.

(My first French Kiss)

In Seagoville, every year they would have a carnival, I was standing in line for a ride when a girl and her sister came behind me. I promised not to say who because we ended up in different clichés in school. However, she allowed me to go around the carnival with them. We had a wonderful time. I had liked her, but never felt there was the same to me. When it came time for them to go home, they had to meet their ride at the end of the street away from the carnival. It was dark, so I came with them. While waiting, the conversation got serious and we began to kiss. All of a sudden, I had her tongue in my mouth. Surprised and embarrassed, I stuck my tongue into her mouth, too. It was amazing. We kissed until her ride came along. This was a one time get together. And though it was a special time in my life, I never told anyone who it was because I did not want anything to happen to her status at school. But, to her, I thank you.

I did not realize these years had many things to cover when I started my blog. I guess I will have to continue it in Blog 12. Until then.....

Blog 12: (cont) 9th grade

As I stated, I felt I had to be the best in everything. I tried not to engage myself to things that did not point to me. I really loved school, anyways. I had been a lifeguard, won district champion in the 500 yard freestyle and 100 yard backstroke. I was named most valuable boy for my first year, and when I was home, I had this wonderful baby boy just waiting to see me. Terri and I were still spending time together outside of school going to many swim meets all over Texas and being in Explorers.

Remember the girl I wrote about braiding her hair and sticking pencils in to hold them as she walked down the hall? She was in almost all my classes in 9th grade and we actually became best friends. She introduced me to two of her friends, and the four of us became a group of know it all's, but also, fun troublemakers. Vanessa, Jeanie, Betsy and I started a bond that has lasted past school years. Jeanie was very mischievous. I was scared of her at first. But, by 10th grade, she and the others opened me up to quit being a do-gooder. It was quite fun. The best thing about it was that we could get away with murder because, in class, we were such ANGELS!

I became close friends with Steven, Terse, Kristi, Jeff, Steve, Joyce, Terry, of course, Terri and many others that shared the same likes as me. I have many stories to tell about everyone of these people. All great, and all life-long. We would be stuck in 9th and 10th grade for quite some time if I told them all. Terri and I attended the National Explorer Congress in Washington, DC, both our 9th and 10th grades to elect our National Officers. What a great and fun experience. At free-times, we were both looking to make new friends from around the country, but we got together at parties, and election time. I did the best I could to be "good", and to be a great role model for little Del (Anthony).

A My entire High School Crush

(The secret crush that never could come true.)

When I became a lifeguard at the swimming pool the summer between my 8th and 9th grade, I met a girl name Joyce-Marie that literally stole my heart... She was very beautiful, nice, and her eyes and smile melted me every time I saw her. She was two years younger than me, so I never said ANYTHING to her. But I would let her and her friends into the pool for free.

I could not wait for summer every year, because I knew she would come swimming. What was my problem that I could not tell her how I felt? Well, Joyce became very popular and, of course, I was type casted in another cliché. I felt that I did not deserve her attention. I thought that if I tried to show my affection to her, it would become a joke at school. BUT, at the pool in the summer, I had a better chance to talk to her without ridicule from others,

The summer that I was going into tenth grade, and Joyce was going into the eighth, Joyce was becoming more beautiful, friendly and popular. I decided that this was my only chance to see how she felt. So, at closing time for the pool, we crossed paths on our bicycles in the park and stopped to talk.

This was the time to ask Joyce to go to Six Flags with me. As a lump came up my throat, I said, "Joyce, would you go to Six Flags with me?" To my surprise, she said, "Yes!" I WAS IN HEAVEN! But about a few days later she came to me and said she could not go.

Very hurt; and I assumed her friends talked her out of it, I could not even ask why. But, it was when we began talking on Facebook a few years back, Joyce told me that it was because she was only an 8th grader and her DAD said no.

Over the last two years of my high school, Joyce just kept becoming more popular, as well as, being picked into our Most Beautiful category and I never told her how I felt at that point because I convinced myself that I was out of her choices. I remember always being smitten every time she passed by or talked to me. I look back know and often wonder what Joyce would have said, had I told her how I felt? I do know now, that it is far too late to find out.

Blog 13: Stories of Billy Boy

For some reason Billy Boy had the feeling that he had higher rights than the rest of us. He and Anna had a relationship similar to mine and Darrell's. But, the boys were forbidden to hit the girls.

(Anna's toast)

One day, Anna was making toast and she began mixing melted butter with apple butter. She was, also, talking on the kitchen phone. I was watching from the living room. When Anna turned around to see the toast, she caught Bill stealing a piece. Without any hesitation, she THREW the butter right onto his face. I was laughing hysterically. But, Anna dropped the phone and ran into the den with Billy following her. I did not see what happened next, but I sure told my parents when they came home and that was not very fun for Bill.

(Lime Green Kool-Aid)

Another time, Anna had a friend coming over to borrow some dish soap. It was green Palmolive. She placed it on the dining room table, then made a pitcher of lime green Kool-Aid. She placed it directly beside the glass of Palmolive. Anna came into the living room with me and sat on the couch. In walks Billy Boy from his room. (You can guess what happened next!) Billy picked up the glass and started drinking it. He took a BIG gulp. His reaction was priceless. Anna never admitted if she did it deliberately or not, but I have my own opinion….. She planned it!

(The Peeping Tom)

One night, one or both girls were in the bathroom getting ready for bed. When they did, both came running out screaming that someone just whistled through the window at them. The dogs WERE barking, so we called the police. It did not take long for the police to arrive with a sniffing dog.

They confirmed that the dog picked up a scent from the window to the alley. But, no one was found. After the police left, Anna, Darrell, and I were afraid to stay in our bedrooms, so we went to our parents bed. There was a small hallway between my parents room and the den. I laid closest to the window looking out through the sashes. Anna was in the middle and Darrell was closest to the hall.

I stared hard outside the window while the other two talked. All of a sudden, Anna started screaming. Darrell joined in harmony. ME? I just started screaming because they were screaming. But, I turned around and saw a shadow in the hallway. They had something in their hand and had it lifted over there head. We screamed even louder.

Out of nowhere, Billy walked into the room "combing his hair!" Then he calmly said, "What is wrong with y'all?" I started crying, Anna began yelling and I think Darrell might have wet his pants! He got in sooo much trouble when my mom got home.

(The Bet)

I have to admit that I was a tattle tell. My parents knew they could leave us because when they got home, I would be pointing at person/ people who did something wrong. I think I proved this when telling the stories about Darrell and me.

One day, Dad, Billy and I were in the den. Dad's chair was in the middle of the room and you had to pass it to go to the bathroom from the couch. I bet Billy Boy that I could get him in trouble. He did not believe me. So, I got up and went into the kitchen and came back in the den passing Bill. I deliberately tripped myself a little and turned to Billy and said, "Dad, Billy is trying to trip me!" My dad responded, "Son, you better leave him alone!"

I waited a couple of minutes and got up to go to the restroom. When I passed Billy, I tripped myself a little harder. I yelled, "Bill quit it!!" My dad warned him again. I stayed in the restroom long enough and came back by Bill again. This time I tripped myself and fell to the floor fake crying. I yelled to dad that Billy did it again and this time it hurt! My dad got up, grabbed his belt and told Bill to go to his room! "VICTORY!!!"

(Bill's friend Choya)

I did not win in every case. Bill's friend, Choya came through the front door and I was playing the piano. I STUPIDLY made a smart remark to him as he passed me. (Wrong Idea) Choya grabbed me, turned me upside down and hooked my belt buckle on the door and left me hanging there. I said, "You think your smart don't ya?" I reached up and simply unbuckled my belt buckle. (Not So Smart Of Me) I came straight down on my head ....BASH!!!! I had a knot on my head for two weeks.

(one story with dad)

When we were still at an age to need a babysitter, Mom would go to work at 3pm and dad would sleep until 6pm and then would go to work. We had an old style refrigerator that was empty in the kitchen. Anna, Darrell, and I decided to play on the ice box. Anna got on top, Darrell got inside on a shelf, and I swung on the door like it was a bus. Anna driving, Darrell in a seat, and me jumping on to catch the bus.

It got too heavy and fell over. Anna and I jumped off, but the door slammed shut with Darrell still inside. The sound of the crash and the screaming woke my dad. He came running into the kitchen and all of us got the ice box upright and got Darrell out. My dad was furious, but, he got even more furious when he realized that he was standing in front of the babysitters in his underwear! Wow, we got a horrible whipping for that stunt!!

(Hoping the best for those involved in Hurricane Harvey and the one about to hit Florida. I pray for you all and I hope these stories got your mind off these disasters for a moment.) Sincerely, Millard

Blog 14: 10th Grade (part one)

(The most important change of my life)

(Metamorphosis)

Hello, Everyone! I'm glad to be back online. My computer crashed and I had to get another computer. Along with that, we have had many worldwide tragedies occurring and I just did not feel right writing during these times, I know they are still going on, but if I do not get back to writing this, I will lose my passion.

Many things happened in my 9th and, mostly, 10th grade that I will be doing it in parts. First, let me say that you please do not judge the people I ran around with. They truly were just close friends. It is what you did not see that would blow your mind, although I am not going to give names. In my 10th grade, I made it a mission to grow up and make adult decisions, while also being a kid when around friends. My nephew was still my first priority of taking care. Good grades at school were my second, swimming third, and girlfriends fourth. Religion was above all, and accepting people for who they were, just came naturally.

49

I was still an active Boy Scout and Explorer. And it was during this time I made a great friend named, Steven. When it came to scouting, we were very close. It was an important part of both our lives. (After graduation, we got into the drinking scene and I will hit upon that later.) But, we have one pretty funny memory while coming home from a camping trip with my brothers.

(Scouts to the rescue)

Billy Boy was driving and we came upon a fire in the land next to the road. It was out of hand and because of the wind, it was spreading quickly. We only saw 2 other men trying desperately to put it out, so our scouting abilities took over and we stopped to help. Our only equipment were our tennis shoes and we began running around frantically stomping out the fire. We did this for what felt like hours until firetrucks FINALLY showed up. They thanked us and we decided that it was our time to leave. However, when we stepped back onto the road, our shoes were sticking to the road, We had been stomping for so long, that the rubber soles of our shoes had melted. One step, and we literally were left standing in our socks. All our shoes were ruined. And the smell of smoke on our clothes made a horrible trip the rest of the way home. But still, proudly, we laughed and laughed as each person gave their story of their adventures. Our shoes were so melted that we had tree sticks, leaves, pecans, etc., all stuck to them.

(Little Anthony was growing fast.)

While I was teaching Anthony (Del) all that I could, he was becoming a proud, but cocky, smart student. He had a great memory. He could spell, do easy math, say kid's poetry, and tell jokes. And he was only 2 years old. One thing that he was really great at was knowing which money was higher. At a football game, my mom was showing him off to a family friend. She said," Del, I will give you a nickel if you tell my friend the story about Mary's Little Lamb." Del immediately said," For just a nickel? I don't want to.". So mom said, "Okay, I will give you a dime!" Del smugly put out his hand and said, "No mam", A QUARTER!!"

(a kid catches everything you say)

Anna was the one to teach Del who people were. She did this by using picture albums, mostly. I would be listening to her teach him and as she pointed all the family out, when she came to Del's father, she would flip the page saying," There's that son-of-a-b$%&&!" Well. one day my mother took Anthony over to his paternal grandmother's home and she had pictures of her children on her wall, (You guessed it!) Del pointed up to a picture on the wall and said, "Look Granny! There's that son-of-a-b***!" Mom was so embarrassed, but his grandmother just said, "That's alright, sometimes he can be one!!"

(Del did not like to share)

In 8th Grade, my sister, Mary, got married to William (Bill) Fisher. With so many Bill's in the family, we started calling Billy Boy, "WOS" and Bill Fisher, "Fish". Well, when Del was 3, we went to eat at the Dairy Queen in Seagoville. I was with Mary and Fish. I ordered Del a corn dog and fries. Well, Fish reached over to Del's plate and said, "Look Del, I got your fries!" So Del mumbled and grabbed a few fries and shoved them into his mouth. We laughed, so I took a fry and Del put a few more in his mouth. Fish and I did this again and by this time, Del had shoved so many fries in his mouth he looked like a chipmunk. We all were laughing so hard and suddenly realized Del was turning red in the face and was crying because he had too many fries in his mouth that he was hardly breathing and could not chew or swallow. I quickly shoved my finger in his mouth and scooped all the fries out. Del cried and cried. But, after that he began sharing his food more generously!!!!!

(Riding The class float for Homecoming)

Every year at football Homecoming, Seagoville would have a parade. The high school classes would make a float based on a certain theme. The theme that year was "The Decades". The sophomores chose "The Gay Twenties" (Ironic). My dad had a Zoot Suit that was his father's.

Ms. Pyland helped us with the guys outfits and I had hand me downs and an old hat that I wore. Vanessa dressed as a flapper along with another girl who danced the Charleston the ENTIRE parade. We had a car from the 20s and it made it look like we were on a picnic. We took 2nd place under the Seniors (who always won). I had a great time!!!!!

(to be continued in Blog 15)

Blog 15: 10th Grade (cont)

(The Championship Year)

Swimming hit my all-time best this year. During this year, I broke and re-broke and held every swim record except for Breaststroke and Butterfly. By the end of the year, I still held 6 records, Our team, both girls and boys won district Champions. Our Explorer scout unit, also, won district and regional champions and during the summer, we went to our first National Explorer Olympics in Colorado. We won the right to go again, 2 years later, and this time it was more exciting. The things that happened that year will be talked about in about three blogs from now.

(A very active year for romance and one-time encounters)

As I said before, I had a girlfriend every year in high school. The girl that I dated this year was very special. She had a special nickname that implied that she had large boobs. I was in heaven. Outside of school, we had a very special bond, but because of my upbringing, we never went past 3rd base. I will say that I considered myself a breast and leg guy. She definitely met both criteria, as well as, was very fun to be with.

However, this year began an array of one-time encounters with other guys. I never looked for them, they would just happened. There was something about nice-looking guys that would hit on…me! It meant nothing to me except keeping my promise about respecting girls. I learned a lot this year concerning sex. (In all aspects of the word.) It made me feel special to be approached, rather than me having to take getting the turn downs. At that time, it did not seem like I was doing anything wrong, but of course, I always felt bad afterwards.

(A very crushing moment.)

Through all the year, Terri was still my closest friend. We had many classes together, swim team, Explorers. the person to talk to when things happened, and my "go to" person for help. Suddenly, she announced that her family was moving to Virginia soon. It ripped my heart out. I was losing my best friend! It got harder to think about the closer the day came. On her last weekend, we were able to purchase some Tickled Pink Wine and we drank the entire bottle, then went to my house to jump on our trampoline one last time.

It was getting late, and I knew our time was coming to an end. In a last ditched effort, and not knowing anything else to try, I proposed to her. I told her it just would not be the same without her. (I know it was stupid looking back on it, but at the time I meant every word!) Terri, of course, said no. I know it was wrong because she immediately got off the trampoline and said she needed to leave. We bid each other one last hug and then she left. I went to my room and cried my heart out. I was in a slump for a very long time. I later heard from her and from that point on, I knew we would be "Besties" for life. And that is how it is to this day!

(Biology…my favorite class)

I had plans to go to college to become a doctor, so Biology was very important to me. A lot happened in that class. Before Terri left, we sat across the room from each other. we had learned finger spelling and some sign language. So, when it came to tests, we were able to hang our hands down beside our desks and spell to each other when we needed help, or just to talk during class.

The teacher was very smart and funny. He did things all the time to make us laugh. He always had the class windows opened so there were many flies. He would be teaching then out of nowhere he would climb up on the shelves, grab a book and follow a fly until he was above it. Then he would drop the book, "BAM", right on top of the fly.

Once a girl fell asleep in class so, without any notice, he took a lid and filled the top with WD40. He told us that when he gave the signal, we were to run toward the door. The teacher laid the lid next to the girl's head, lit it on fire and yelled, "Fire, Fire!!!" we all jumped up and the girl opened her eyes, saw the flame, screamed and hit the lid off her desk while screaming. Flames flew everywhere! No one was hurt, but if he did that now, he would be fired and probably sued!

When we started labs, I was partnered with one of our class beauties. I was in heaven. It was fun because when it came to dissecting things, she would cringe and make squeaky noises and would only touch the critter with her fingernails. I did not mind because I loved doing the cutting up and making jokes. (Not to mention being able to sit beside her for half the year.)

On one assignment, we had to look through a telescope, find a paramecium, and then draw and label the parts all to a perfect frame. The teacher would go around the room measuring the frames and labels with a ruler, and if he did not like it, he would tear it up and you had to start over. The tables had students on both sides, and we had finally gotten a perfect picture. Suddenly, all these sprinkles of water came from the other side of the table and it ruined our paper. I looked up at the guys on the other side and yelled, "I bet you think that was soooo funny, don't you?" Then, from behind them, the teacher popped up with a spray bottle and just started laughing!! I was fuming! He came around, looked at our paper and tore it up. I was about to go ballistic! He came back to us and whispered, "I will give you an "A", don't worry!"

(Blog 16 and 17 will be my junior year, my mom, and goodbye, Del and the many hijinks of Jeanie)

Blog 16: Summer, 11th Grade

This is a picture of my girlfriend during most of my Junior and Senior years. (The girl, not the clown!)

I was a horrible boyfriend, This is at Six Flags on the day of the Junior Prom. I convinced my girlfriend that we could have a great full day at Six Flags instead of a few hours at a Prom, for the same price or cheaper. You see I won, but I'm sure I ruined her dreams of the Prom. We did have a great day, but I never forgave myself for doing that.

(A secret about Darrell)

In my last trimester of 10th grade, during the last week for the seniors, I was getting rumors that my brother, Darrell, was going to fail. I told you earlier that Darrell was extremely lazy when it came to school. Many times just missing school entirely. Plus, the teachers had problems with him in class making noises,(even snoring). He was not teacher's favorite!

I went to the teacher that was failing him. She was going to be having me in class my Senior year, and she knew that I was a good student. First, I tried the begging trick and she would not have any of it. I even tried promising to work double hard in her class when I had her. But, still no budging her.

Finally, I tried reverse psychology. After she told things he did in class that she considered unbearable, I assured her that Darrell definitely would not go to summer school, and would be just as happy coming back to school to HER class again. At the time, she said if he preferred that then so be it.

A few classes later, I saw her running down the hall pretty quick. By the the end of the day, Darrell told me that the teacher had "found a test that Darrell never got credit for and it just happened to be an 'A' which was enough credit to change his grade from an 'F' to a 'D' and he deserved to graduate. My brother never knew I pleaded for his mercy and I really do believe that the teacher gave it a second thought of having him in her class again!

(Being the only driver in the home.)

Again, I have to tell on Darrell for this to make sense. When he was a Sophomore, he took driver's education class 3 times and failed all of them ONLY because the classes were at 7am and he would not get up and go!! So, he decided to wait until he was 18 and he could just take the test and driving course. He knew he could pass it, but my father refused to let him drive until he got his license. Of course, I got my trainer's license at 15, and my real license at 16. (Remember, I had already been driving for 3 years.)

This was the beginning years that my mother's health started interfering my life. If she felt she needed to go to the emergency room, my father would refuse to take her and my brother, Bill could instantly come up with a reason why he could not take her. My dad would never let her call an ambulance because it was too expensive due to how many times she felt she had to go or she would die, only to be sent back home.

This left me being the only person she could get to take her. I would be called out of class (as an emergency) to take her to the hospital. Without going through her illnesses, all I say is this became a habit. It did not affect my 10th grade, but as I will tell you soon, it demolished my 11 Grade.

(Anthony getting older and smarter)

(I will have to continue this on blog 17th, but this will be done in a day soon.)

Blog 17: Changes again, grade drops, living on my own

(Becoming self-sufficient)

As told previously, I had a girlfriend from my Junior and most of my Senior year. She was great. I was trying to be a very good boy, but things did happen with others. It was far and few between, but the guilt was daily. I was putting her on a pedestal so there were times I just had the urge like other teenagers. It was the year I lost my virginity with a female. But, I really did care for my girlfriend very much.

I gave her a promise ring and really meant it. But, I could not be true to her. I knew somewhere, even though I fought hard, down the line I was going to slip and I did. I prayed and prayed for strength, but the devil made it very hard. I kept wondering why I was put in this situation, even with God watching over me and had things in control.

This was the year that my mom went into the hospital 32 times, and I was her fallback for taking and picking her up at the hospital. This created it hard to do my studies, swim practice twice a day, (and with dad working nights), feeding myself, as well as caring for Anthony. I was so close to Anthony. One night, coming back home from watching a football game in a full station wagon, I was trying to get Anthony to talk, I kept trying to get him to say Uncle Millard. Out of nowhere, and very clearly trying, he pointed at me and said, "Babasata" (babysitter). Everyone in the car heard him. That was the first word he had ever completed, even before "mommy". I loved him like my own son.

After Terri left, I leaned on my other friends. If felt easy to hide my true self, by separating my friends during the day. I had my school friends, my swim team friends, my scout friends, and such. By having no one really looking after me, I could come and go as I pleased. I had goals, but they were very hard to strive for when my entire week was set for me in advance.

(Surviving)

When it came to my school, scouts, Explorers, and just daily activities, my dad was dead set to refuse helping pay for things. That included clothes, as well. Dad, every two weeks, would place lunch money for two weeks in a certain drawer, He gave us just enough to buy the basic lunch (only). He said that was all we needed. I realized that Darrell was taking more money than his share, so I would take my portion and pay for lunch passes because dad told us if the money was used before two weeks, we would go the rest of the time with no lunch. I had no choice but to do two things. First, I needed a job during school, and second, When dad would come home drunk, after he fell asleep, I would steal money from his pants. He always thought he drank more and that He spent the money.

I worked during Christmas season at Woolco at Big Town. I also worked at Dairy Queen and Jack-In-The-Box. I kept my lifeguard job every summer. I would buy my school clothes twice a year. Once, at the end of summer, and second, when I got my tax refund. Many times, I would have to use my money for food to feed Anthony. There were lots of times I would have Vienna sausages or potted meat for dinner.

With my mom being unable to work, she filed for social security in my 9th grade. She did not get accepted for two years. When she finally received it, they gave backpay to the date she filed. When you have children under 19 years old, the social security has to give the children compensation, also. So, Anna, Darrell and I received back checks, also. And Darrell and I received monthly checks until we turned 19, My checks were $ 75. This enabled me to stop working while going to school.

My back pay check was close to $1600. Dad took all the checks and demanded that we sign them over to him. He would give us 10%. I refused to sign mine until dad agreed I could buy a car, and have enough money to participate in outdoor activities. I was very serious, and dad finally came to an agreement. I also made it clear that I got to keep my entire monthly check because I was taking care of myself. I won. But, he quit leaving us lunch money, too.

I bought a 1965 Dodge Dart for $300. I had it for 3 years. I was so proud of it, even though it was 12 years old, ate gas and oil for lunch. But, it was mine. It could not be taken from me and I was able to get to the places I needed to go. I came and went whenever I wanted but I still had many obligations. No one ever forgets their first car.

(Losing Salutatorian)

My Junior year classes were very easy for me. I had A's in all my classes. But, in the second trimester, my mom pulled me out of class many times to take her, or pick her up, from the hospital. It was always during my 3-5 classes that this would happen. When I got my report card, I received 3 B's, Like I said, I was definitely an A student. When I asked my teachers how I got B's, they all replied that there was a rule that if a student missed more than 5 days in a class, they automatically drop a grade. Though I held it against her, I never told my mom that she cost me my chances for Valedictorian or Salutatorian (This may sound like an excuse, but it is the truth.) At that point, I took matters into my own hands. To me, mom was just a person in the house that needed attention and I was not going to let her tell me what to do on the days that she was at home and not the Hospital.

(I will try to finish High School in Blog 18, but this was when the fun began and I have many stories)

61

Blog 18: Junior and Senior Years

(Welcome Back)

I need to start this blog off by making it clear that my sister, Anna, was not a bad mother and just ditched Anthony on me. I am very proud of her for trying so hard, with no help from my parents, to make a life for her and Anthony. She was suppose to graduate in 1975, but because she got pregnant, the school made her leave. To my surprise, she made the decision to finish high school. Suddenly, she became a senior my junior year. I was amazed because she could have taken a GED but she chose to graduate.

Anna moved back home, so it made it easier to care for Anthony, She got jobs to take care of them and she paid a woman to care for Anthony until one of us could get him. She graduated in 1978. Again, I was very proud of her. But, there was a period when she dated the father of the most popular boy in my class. Little did she know, it caused a BIG deal in my class, and it created a problem between the boy and me. (Even though I had nothing to do with the situation and Anna was old enough to date his father.) But, you know kids, they embarrassed the boy and pushed him to pick on me. Since I had known the boy since 4th grade, we were able to settle things privately. I forget why, but Anna did move out and again I tried to help with Anthony as much as possible.

(Goody-two shoes?)

In every group of friends, there is always an instigator. At school, our instigator was Jeanie. We knew that because our group was considered the Goody-two shoes. We got away with murder. But, our mayhem was usually innocent. It was great because we got away with murder. Jeanie could convince me to do anything. I will be telling you many stories about Jeanie in a moment.

We learned to manipulate the teachers. Vanessa, Betsy and I were chosen for the National Honor Society our junior year. There were only 7 Juniors selected. Always having the need to be in charge, at the end of our junior year, we voted for the Honor Society officers for our Senior year. With only 7 of us, we only needed 4 votes to win. I got with Vanessa and Betsy and we all made an agreement that we would vote me for President, Vanessa for Vice-President, and Betsy for Secretary. We only needed one more vote to solidify our plan. We talked it over and chose a student that we knew would not want an office. I made a deal with her and our plan was set. WHAT A SHOCK! GUESS WHO THE OFFICERS WERE? I take the blame, but we got away with rigging the votes.

(The summer)

I had the opportunity to be the pool manager at the Boy Scouts summer camps. I was able to do it for a month when I got a call from my sister. Mary was pregnant and Bill Fish was going to be out on a job for a few weeks and they wanted me to come to Colorado to be with Mary while Bill was busy. I agreed. When I came back home, my manager position had been replaced. Luckily, something happened at the city pool and they were in need of an assistant manager/lifeguard to finish the summer and I got the job. But, the week before coming back from Colorado, our Explorer group had won the right to go to the

National Explorer Olympics for the second time. I drove to the event from Mary's house.

(Can you get drunk on vanilla extract?)

While we were competing, we decided we wanted to party one night but none of us were old enough to buy liquor. Smart Millard knew that extracts had alcohol, so I convinced everyone to pitch in to buy them with cokes. I say to this date, DO NOT DO THAT!!!!! None of us even got a buzz, it tasted nasty, and about half of us got sick. But, on the last night of the games, we were invited to a real party and some of us went. My brother, Darrell, decided to be the bartender. My best swimming friend and I went overboard. We got so drunk! At one point, I was talking to my friend, who was passed out and suddenly he threw up all over me. To sober us up, Darrell and others tried walking us around the dormitory, but no results.

They got us back to our room and hoped we would sleep it off before my mom and the other adults found out. We were wasted! We were so sick, that they had to call the doctor in to look at us. He gave us suppositories to help with the nausea. My friend put the wrapped pill in his mouth and was trying to eat it. He started yelling, "Give me a crash helmet. I going to hell for all my sins!" Of course, my mom had to call Mary and Bill to come from Denver to pick me up. They put me in my car to wait for them to come. The rest had to get to the airport to catch their flight. However, my friend was still too drunk when it was time to leave and the airport would not let him fly. So, my mom and he had to stay at the airport until they were given permission to fly. That was the worst drunk I have ever had and, though I became a drinker, I never let myself get that far again! It seemed liked forever until my sister and brother got there to take me home. They put me to bed and I slept a full day.

(I promise Blog 19 will finish school. Even if I go over 1000 words. it will cover The rest of my senior year and the hijinks of Jeanie)

Blog 19: Trying to leave my mark, Hijinks with Jeanie

(Will everyone know your name)

I forgot to add on my last blog that while we were at the Olympics, our co-ed volleyball team won third and I made the top 16 in Tennis. Just FYI!

I wanted to be known, not necessarily popular, but remembered. I served on every class council from 7th grade to Senior, except my Junior year, but was Jr High Student Council President, I was Parliamentarian in Junior High National Honor Society, rode on the Sophomore Homecoming float, was swimming co-captain my sophomore year and captain my junior and senior year, I was swim team Beau my junior and senior year, lettered all four years of high school in swimming, Rookie of the year 8th grade, most valuable boy swimmer all 4 high school years, choir 4 years, wrote our senior class song, drew the cover of our senior annual (with help from Vanessa), produced and directed the senior skit for senior day, President of the high school National Honor society, etc. If it brought attention to me, I was in it. I was very vain. But, not to the point of being friends with everyone i could. I was not trying to be better than others, but I loved attention.

My senior year was filled with so many things that happened. I, also, became an Eagle Scout. Many people do not know this, there are actually ranks higher than Eagle Scout. For every six months service and receiving five additional merit badges, gives you PALMS. The first is Bronze, next is Silver, and the third is Gold. Then it starts over again. I finished my scouting years with four Palms, forty-seven merit badges, and one of the highest ranked Eagles in Dallas. I went on to serve as an adult supervisor until I was twenty-seven. The stories you hear about scouting are far and few, most are outright lies. I loved camping, teaching, and being a comrade for the boys I worked with. Nothing else even crossed my mind. This is getting ahead of myself, so back to school.

(If you don't succeed, try something else!)

At the first of each year, we would have fund drives. One was to simply go door to door asking for donations. When our group realized that Seagoville was swamped with beggars, I came up with the idea to go to another community. We decided which school area would have the most money and we went there. Without outright lying, we would tell the people that we were "seniors at the school" and we would point towards the high school with our hands. We were getting tons of donations …until.….we came to a house of a swimmer that I knew. While someone was telling the parent of our plight, I started trying to get them to be quiet. Our cover was blown! However, the swimmer's mother was so impressed with us that she gave us five dollars anyway. We came back to our school with the most money and out class sponsor was stunned when we told her what we did. (It worked, though!)

We did another fundraiser by selling Hummel plaques. The student with the most sold would receive fifty dollars. I was asking everyone I came across to buy one. They were five dollars each. Near the end of the sell, I found out that it was between another student and me for most sells. I got desperate. So, I went to other students and asked them how many they sold. If it was less than ten, I would convince them to let me turn the names in on my list and then I would give them the plaques when they came in.

I was not in it for the money, I was in it to WIN! So, being confident, but not for sure, I bought ten myself, counting on getting my fifty dollars back. When it was over, I had over 125 plaques. It was announced that I won and second place had only sold somewhere in the nineties. But, I did what it took to win, and that was my goal!!!

(Hijinks with Jeanie and the rest of us)

Jeanie helped to bring me out of my "goody two-shoes" character. She had a mischievous look that could convince me to do any thing. She would do many things and soon, we both plotted many things. I only have enough room to tell a few stories, though.

One time, we had to stop by my house before we went somewhere. I cannot remember why, but she was in a dress. While waiting to leave, we decided to jump on our trampoline. When Jeanie started bouncing, her dress skirt would pop up like a parachute. I started laughing, not because of the parachute, but for the fact that she did not have any panties on and she was flashing me and the entire neighboring houses.

At Halloween, our group decided to go to the Senior Costume Party as the Addams Family. It was awesome because we had all the main characters. I went as Lurch, Vanessa as Uncle Fester (first prize winner), Cheryl was Gomez, Betsy was Morticia, Jeanie was Grand mamah, Teresa was Pugsley. I had our convertible and so we went to Buckner Blvd and started egging all the pedestrians we past. We deliberately missed them, but got very close to scare them.

Later that year, Jeanie and I decided to audition for the Six Flags shows. We were too scared to audition alone, so we did the duet, "You Don't Bring Me Flowers" by Barbra Streisand and Neil Diamond. When we got to the auditions, we were the second ones to arrive. It was at the SMU Auditorium. It was a full house.

When we got on stage, we were a bit nervous. They started the music and then the inevitable happened.....Jeanie choked. No, Jeanie literally choked. She started, "You don't bring me flowers. You don't sing me love…UUGGHH, UUGGHH!" I could have died if it was not so funny. Without skipping a beat, she asked if we could start over. You could hear laughter in the Auditorium. The judges said yes and we got through the song. Noone could leave the stage faster. Needless to say, we did not get a callback.

Before the audition, we went to my house to practice one day. As we came into the house, I directed Jeanie to go through the kitchen to my room because it was the only clean room in the house. I closed rhe front door and turned around to see Jeanie back in the living room with her hands on her face and quite shaken up. She said there was a RAT in the kitchen eating our dog;s food. I said that we had mice, but not rats.

After shutting the front door, I went ahead of Jeanie to assure her that it was a mouse. But, to my embarrassment, it WAS a RAT!!!! I leaped at it, stomping my feet, and even hit a broom near the rat. It simply looked at me and slowly waddled toward the corner of the the bar and wall to an extremely small hole and that rat squeezed right through the hole like I was not bothering it at all.

I grabbed Jeanie, who was still in shock, and took her to my room. I was so embarrassed that I made a promise to clean the living room, dining room, kitchen, part of the hall that went to my room, and my bathroom. I swore to keep them clean until I went to college. I asked dad to buy some rat traps and to my surprise, each time I could get a trap set, a trap would go off. In no more than an hour, we had captured at least fifteen rats. It made me sick to my stomach.

One day at lunch, we decided to leave the school grounds (which was a no-no) and go to the Dairy Queen. I was in the convertible, again, and I sneaked my car around behind the football field. There were about five of us. We no sooner got away from the school when Jeanie sat up on the back of the car and started yelling loudly, "Call the Principal, We are skipping school!!" By the time we came back, our principal was in the parking lot looking around. We immediately turned back around to the front of the school and I dropped everyone off. I then took my car and hid it behind the football field and sneaked across the field back to the lunch room. Whew! We made it back without getting caught.

For Christmas that year, we decided to go caroling. we went to Pleasant Grove and wanted to sing to the couple that every year decorated their entire yard (which was on a hillside.) We knocked on the door and then started singing (VERY BADLY). The couple asked if we were going to sing anymore? We said yes, and they immediately ushered us to the side of the house and had us sing there. I could sense the discomfort, and as we started again, we were sooooo off key. I started yelling for us to stop, but they kept going. We no sooner finished the song that the people thanked and said they needed to go back in the house. (How Rude) We stood there not knowing what just happened, but finally took the hint and left.

(This blog is too big, so I will have to finish it (FINALLY) on Blog 20!)

Blog 20: The End of High School, The job of being a lifeguard, the tricks for getting 'A's

(The Tricks for getting 'A's)

It was a known fact that teachers had to meet a quota of so many A, B, and C students to keep their jobs. Each one had special ways of involving the certain signals to help us pass. I am going to tell the secrets without giving names. I loved Math and Science and they were true teachers, but many others had tricks that if you paid attention, an 'A' was easy.

One teacher would give you a practice test the day before the real one. He said it was not required to turn it in. The trick was that many of the practices ended being the Real test, or almost the test. It was very easy to figure out.

Another teacher was known to use a light projector for us to write the notes down. During the writing, anytime there was something that was going to be on the test, she would make some kind of noise to signal us to remember this. It was every test. She did this the entire year.

There was a teacher who for an entire year only had us read and study the same two chapters. He never made us take tests, but he would just have us read or respond about those chapters.

Somehow, I got put in a class as the only student as a senior on a teacher's class break. On top of that, she had two student assistants that happened to be two my best friends. The teacher would give me my assignment and then leave to the teacher's lounge. The assistants would be working with the earlier classes work and somehow, I would find a copy of an 'A'. I would do my work and then we would sit around and talk. This happened with the tests, as well.

The best thing about this class was that it was the one that we always had fire alarm drills. We would close all the window skirts and hide in the farthest corner of the class that could not be seen by the hall monitor. When the drill was over and students started back down the hall, we would open back the windows and put the room back in order. We did not participate in a single fire drill that year! Many times the teacher would bring us back cold drinks.

(How did you spend your last day of school?)

If you had an 'A' or 'B' you did not have to take finals. So Vanessa and I were asked to drive around Dallas looking for the record or background music for our senior class song. This was the day before finals, we were suppose to be there. The teacher wrote a note that our grades had already been computed and to please excuse us to do this. For some reason, we decided to spend the entire day away from school, even though we had bought the song within the first 30 minute. (Now, looking back, I wish we had come back to school.)

(The time as a lifeguard at the swimming pool.)

Four and a half years as a lifeguard at the city pool was such a great job. I got paid to hang around the pool getting tanned and having a good time on my break or when I worked up front. At first, it created a problem because I wore these real tight yellow shorts when not on the stand and I would take them off when on the guard stand or tanning. I wore my racing swim suit under the shorts. They were very revealing and some people were offended. I said that I had races after work sometimes and I had to be ready. I, also, had them look at swimmers world magazine and it showed only the same suits. I won, but still had times when people opposed. But, I think I got more compliments of my tan and swim body than what I wore. After the first year, it really never mattered.

It is true that you get noticed more when you are a lifeguard. I was one of the nice guards who would let swimmers break rules as long as they asked me first so I could keep an eye on them. Sometimes I would get change out of the register and have people play songs. But, the pool had a small building that we would do our cleaning and flushing of the pool. It was not unusual for us to get down in the drain area and take showers while the fresh water was filling the pool. I will mention that in the time I worked there, other things happened in there also, but I do not need to go into details. (Use your imagination!)

(Camping at the Guadalupe River)

Both the swim team and the Explorers liked camping in New Braunfels on the Guadalupe River. Instead of regular tents, we had tent hammocks to sleep in. We set up two regular tents for my mom, our food, and emergencies. We would go down the river in inter-tubes and camped right at a bridge that had a small waterfall. At night, we would take bath/showers there. All of us were very close both in swimming and explorers, so it was not uncommon that we would skinny dip. Of course, only under the bridge in the deep water. If we showered under the waterfall, we had our swimsuit on.

One Easter break my best friend on the guys swimming team and I decided to camp at the river for the week. Instead of a tent, we decided to camp under a small cave made from rock. It was just deep enough for us to have shelter because it was suppose to rain during the week. The only other people that were there was a couple camping in their truck. They invited us over one evening for a small party, I had just turned 18, but my friend was still 17. (I guess I should admit that it was the same friend that got drunk at the National Olympics.)

They offered us Wild Turkey whiskey. The next morning, we both were sick and had horrible headaches, but when our new friends asked us to take a raft down the river, we were ready and went along. On the way to the top of the river, they told us the girl did not know how to swim and he had already started drinking beer. I insisted that the girl wear a life preserver. I was right, we did not even make it over the first falls and got sucked under and our boat flipped. (Ice cold water sobers you up very quickly). I came up and immediately went for the girl, while my friend went for the raft and paddles. The guy was coasting along on top of his beer cooler.

The couple decided they better not go again, but they would bring us back our tubes so we could go on. It did rain the night before, so the gates to the river were slightly opened and the water was going fast. It was a blast. What usually took four hours to do, only took forty minutes. Even so, the sun was out and we were lobsters. Our friends had left, and it started raining very hard. There was a tree swing that we played on and the current would send us down the river.

A park ranger appeared and told us that we could stay in the cave, but the car would be flooded in if we did not move it immediately. My friend got in the car and the ranger and I stood in water where the road was so he could maneuver the car in the right direction. As we were talking, we suddenly heard a car honking because my friend was barreling straight at us. To be dramatic, I say that I grabbed the ranger, which I think we grabbed each other, and leaped out of the way. As my friend went past us, he drowned us with a wave of water. I considered it hilarious but I do not think the ranger was as delighted! To get back to the cave, we were going to have to stroll through water, so we decided to move our things to the front of the park. We realized that the rain was not going to end, so we decided to leave.

However, the car was flooded and would not start so we had to wait a day. We were out of food and had to sleep in the car. Our ranger came by the next morning to check on us and thoughtfully brought us a slab of venison jerky. It was so nasty that we both chose to starve instead. That morning, his car started and we decided to leave. Our first stop was a restaurant for breakfast and coffee. It was then that my friend realized he had lost his glasses when the raft flipped, so I had to drive home. It was the best AND worst camping trip at the river.

I am sure everyone is ready for me to move on to stories after high school. But, Blog 21 is going to be a smorgasbord of a few details I failed to mention. I have been good about not telling sad stories, so I am going to talk about a few. (Blog 21 on its way)

Blog 21: The leftovers

(The last of my childhood surprises.) (Living in a house with no heat, oven, hot water or a stove)

When I was ending eighth grade, mom went through all these things that she could be allergic to. Immediately, she was allergic to perfumes, deodorants, cigarettes, shampoos, insecticide, and natural gas. Everthing in our house was run on natural gas and not electric. We had to turn the gas off, even though we could not afford to put in electric. We could only use dove soap, unscented laundry soap, no scented deodorants or shampoos, and no colognes. This went on for four years.

At first, we had nothing, but slowly my grandmother bought us a two-coil electric stove, then came a small electric oven that hardly anything could fit in, and finally a microwave that dad would only use for heating water or making popcorn. I showered at the swimming pool, ate at Griffs or ate potted meat or Vienna sausage sandwiches at night. My only major meal usually was at school lunch or doing dinner runs from the swimming pool.

For Christmas, we were given electric blankets and small electric heaters for our bed rooms. Bill Fish had some extra carpet pieces that we put around the house to not walk on cold floors.. We had a bad case of roaches and mice. But, we could not use sprays to kill them. When the city would go around town fogging for mosquitoes or other bugs, they had to call my mom ahead of time so she could leave town for a couple of days. We went from THE party house, to THE horror house. My true friends tried to understand, but there still were embarrassing times if mom smelled ANYTHING she thought she was allergic from. Boy she knew how to milk a scene!

Even so, mom was always the chosen adult to be in charge of us for outdoor activities. Everyone loved her. I felt bad for her having to give up so much, but it meant us, too. Finally, my uncle gave dad the money to buy an air conditioner/ heater my senior year. By then, I was doing a fairly good job of keeping the main part of the house clean. When my brother, Bill WOS, and I would argue about him not doing something to keep the house cleaned, he would answer, "Okay Susie Homemaker!"

(The Party Glasses)

After parties or swim meets, I usually had our station wagon. I could carry four couples. We usually went to Crawford Park in Pleasant Grove to go parking. Each couple would take a seat, we had three and the fourth would be in the suitcase area. On two separate occasions, my friend, yes the one from the river story, lost or broke his glasses. Once, because he was tall and had to open his door. Well, we got spotted by a police car, so we all rushed to look neat in the car. I quickly shut his door and "CRUNCH", broken glasses.

On another time, we all had blankets and went down by the water. My friend actually took his glasses off again and placed them on his blanket. When it was time to leave, he stood up, grabbed his blanket and "SWOOSH" his glasses went flying into the tall grass and lost them again. The next time I saw his mother, she said she was going to have to think twice about him going with me because he always seemed to lose his glasses and it was beginning to be too expensive to let him go!

There is still so much I left out, but it is time to begin my adult life, so we begin next Blog 22 starting with the true partying me!!

Blog 22: An important message from me. and one last story of high school

(How this picture became so fun)

In my Senior year, both my sisters were pregnant. Mary had her son in February,1979, and Anna was due in August. Anna had set up with Olan Mills for a family picture when she was seven months pregnant. When it was time for the shooting, I was the only one available, so we agreed to go and not lose her deposit.

When we arrived the photographer assumed we were man and wife and took pictures that made you think the same. When the pictures were ready, we thought they were great so we kept the originals. This was my favorite and I remember that it was a blast doing it!

(Sometimes you just cannot win.)

I was still dating Tina when the Senior Prom came around. This time I was going to take her and signed us up as coming. Tina and I shared my larger Senior locker. About two weeks before the prom, she was absent from school and I became concerned, but her sister told me not to call. Well, Tina's best friend sat behind me in homeroom.

Wednesday, we always reported to our homeroom and her friend handed me a letter to read, and she said she promised Tina she would not give it to me until then. It was a very sad, disturbing letter telling me she ran away to her real mother in Maryland, not because of me, but because her father had been abusing her physically, mentally, and sexually and she could not take it anymore. She did not want me to know she was leaving because it might cause her father and I to try to talk her in to staying or him thinking I helped her leave.

I was crushed and angry. I had to take our names off the prom list. That same day her father called me and told me he knew I helped her escape. He told me to be watching behind me because one day he would be there and would kill me. I tried to tell him I just found out, but he did not believe me. He again threatened me and I hung up. It took me weeks to come back to my senses. I got a call from Tina to tell me she was sorry. I told her it was the right thing to do and I was glad she had the courage to leave. I never heard from her again for about eight years.

(Breaking News)

Because of all the molesting allegations going around this week,(2018 Me Too Movement), I felt obligated to tell everyone that after the day I told my dad, while holding Anthony in my arms, that there will be no more and that if I found out he attempted to to try anything with him it would be his last, I started making it my goal to fight for children's rights. But after I graduated and had nephews and a niece that I wanted to watch over, this made me more concern. Although it took me fifty years to talk about it, which I now know was wrong, I took it in a different direction.

However, children need to be monitored and told more by parents and adults in charge that these type of actions are wrong. Predators use the tactic of making you feel special and/or tell you they would never get to be in your life again. I had the same reaction that most victims have. I was made to feel special, I loved my father and did not want to lose that love, and it was something I did not want the blame. Even when my doctor and the others were never in my life again, I was embarrassed to admit it. For years I kept people wondering and kids can be very evil when they do not know the truth, but have an opinion. And lastly, most of the time you enjoy it. (Boy, that was hard to say.)

I put it so far back in my mind, I learned how to walk. talk, react, and kept myself in a group of people that left others...... just not sure. I went MANY years not even truly knowing how I felt. And, once you become an adult, it frees you to be yourself. I had to make decisions that should never have been there. It was very confusing. I was taught that you honor women, but was also thinking it was nothing wrong with other guys. It meant nothing to me. This is where I am in my life at eighteen. I beg everyone to have a talk with your kids about it. They have a voice.

This was not what I was going to say in this blog, but I just felt it needed to be said! I am sending this blog out like this, and will get to the nitty gritty of my party days in the next blog, which I will post on November 19th) hopefully in 2 blogs. Thank-you for allowing me to post it and if you have never SHARED my blog before, please do it this time!

Blog 23: My last free summer, 1st semester in college, the need for a job, sharing an apt, 2nd semester debacle

(Being able to part my hair for the first time.)

(I could be myself!)

Even though I felt like I raised myself through High School, it was different after school was over. I was the assistant manager for the swimming pool, and since I was old enough to buy alcohol, I was asked many times to be the provider for parties after the pool closed. I received a full swim scholarship to two Northern schools. After reading the requirements for the scholarships, I realized I would not be able to stay focused on my pre-medicine classes and also swim.

The scholarship I received for being highest ranking boy was limited to one semester and you had a list of schools you could use it at. I chose

Saint Edward's University in Austin. It was ranked fifteenth in the country for a medicine program. Yes, it is a private Catholic school and I was Baptist, but that did not mean much except for choir. It was a requirement to sing in the choir at mass every other Sunday. That was very awkward!!

Most of my friends had already begun their adult lives, as well. Because I worked at the pool and was still active in Boy scouts, I usually was the oldest. I had already befriended a guy named Steve. Since he was active in scouting, too, we hung around together on my days off, or Saturday nights because the pool did not open until 1 pm on Sunday. I liked Michelob and Coors beer or Seagrams seven and seven. Even though I partied with others, also, little did I know that Steve could out drink all of them.

Since Steve was still under age, we would drink at his house with his parents inside. We played the game where you used a can opener at the bottom of the can. you would suck out all the air in the can, turn it upside down, then someone would give the signal to pop the top of the can. The suction would shoot the beer down your throat. Obviously, the person who could finish first without spilling any out won the round. We could get drunk very quickly. When the beer was finished we would get into my car, go to Pleasant Grove on Buckner Blvd, and go girl hunting.

Once Steve was drunk, he would become this horn dog. Not a car could pass with girls in it that he did not try to get them to stop and talk with us. Sometimes it worked, and sometimes it did not. But, it was never boring either way. We always stayed out late and we never came home sober. But, that is just part of the night. After dropping Steve at home, I would go back out by myself. These trips never turned out lonely. I knew where to go, and instead of me trying to pick someone up, I just had to wait and I would be the one picked up. I never told Steve because I enjoyed our trips and parties and I never wanted to lose that friendship.

(The day we got caught in a horrible storm that included a wind twister)

There was one day that we were going to start partying a little early and was on the highway heading to get beer. The skies got really dark and a major storm began about a mile from Buckner. I could barely see the road in front of me. We pulled under a bridge, and in a few minutes we saw things being blown across the highway in a circular motion. (even a trash can!) My grandmother lived about five miles away, so I decided to go there and get out of the storm. Back then, Jim Miller Road had a big drop in the road that flooded when it rained. To get to my grandmother, we HAD to go through it. I started at the top of the hill and sped up to keep a forward motion continuing through the water. We passed a Cadillac right when we hit the water. I was in my little 1963 Dodge Dart.

As we passed the Cadillac, it drenched us with water. Then the reverse pressure from my car did the same thing to them. Since I started my speed at the top of the hill, I still had good forward momentum as I went through the water. But, our splash to the Cadillac slowed it down and it came to a stop in the middle of the water. As we passed it, and its engine stopped, Steve and I in unison yelled, "Midasize it!!!" The engine was still running, but we coasted through the water. Being the scouts that we were trained, I pulled over to make sure the other car had made it across. We smiled and waved and made it to my grandmother's house right before it began raining hard again.

I went to start my car but it was flooded anyway. We had to wait for it to dry out. My grandmother, being the loving person I always knew, made us some sandwiches and tea, so we spent another thirty minutes or so and finally got back to our party mission. We took a different way back to Steve's house and made it without incident. Onward to start the party. Even though there never were many people, we always had a blast.

I did party with the pool employees, swimmers home for summer break, and sometimes alone. It was now time to get ready for college. I shall start my next blog with this story.

Blog 24: Starting college, surprise roommate, breaking up officially with Tina, etc.

(I am running out of young pictures and since this is a continuation, I will use the same picture.)

(College orientation)

Two weeks prior to my first college semester, the freshmen had orientation. It was mandatory. Not only did we meet all together, they put us in groups so we were sure to meet other freshmen. I saw it as a good idea because I loved meeting people. The group I was placed in had a great variety of characters and we had a blast. We finally found ourselves grouping up at night also. Partying was definitely something we all had in common.

Now, remember this was a catholic school and I am Baptist. I found out why they did not have a swim team! They turned the indoor swimming pool into this cool bar. It had made the pool floor into a double level flat wooded floor with a bar down in the deep level and a dance floor in the shallow end. Sitting booths, tables, conversation areas and another bar were around the pool at ground level. It is still my favorite designed bar of all time. And it was priced for the college kids budget.

(The Talent show)

I was already placed in my dorm room, but did not have a roommate yet. The school had two men's dorms. One had air condition and the other did not. Since I had a roommate, I could afford the air conditioned dorm. I waited to set up my side of the room until I met my roommate. He was a junior and was expected on the weekend before classes started. That Saturday night, the freshmen had a Talent Contest and each group HAD to do something. The winning group won fifty dollars and second place got twenty-five dollars.

Our group used my idea from high school to do two quick skits from the Carol Burnett show. They were really funny and everyone participated. I do not have to tell you that we won, nor what we did with the money. Correct, we went to the bar and partied hardy! I was flat-faced and could hardly stand as I headed back to my room. Now, can you guess what happened next? That is right! I had a roommate!!!

(My first meeting with my roommate!)

When I entered my dorm room, I was greeted by three guys. It was quite obvious that I was drunk. Two of the guys left, and my roommate and I officially introduced ourselves. He was a Junior and had been in this room for the past two years and that he was well known at the campus. I was nauseated so I did not say much. We talked about the talent show and party. While we did, he had pulled out this bottle that had a spout. He pulled out a bag, matches, and a bottle of tequila. He then put towels under the door.

I inquired from my roommate as to what he was doing with all these things. He simply said that he could keep me from having a horrible hangover. I was excited about that, so I watched as he poured the tequila into the bottom of the bottle, which he called a bong. The bottle had a pipe attached and he packed some "chopped up tobacco" in the bowl of the pipe. He said all I had to do was place my mouth in the hole at the top of the bottle, light the tobacco while I inhaled, and then hold my breathe as long as I could. I had nothing to lose, so I did it. Nothing really happened so I did it again. This time my head was spinning and I started laughing. He then told me I experienced my first pot from a bong.

By this time, I was ready to go to bed. With my head spinning, I could not go directly to sleep. But, when I did, I had hallucinations that you could not believe. This went all night long and when I woke up, my mouth felt like it was stuffed with cotton. I was starving. BUT, I was not sick or hungover! It was unbelievable. When my roommate woke up, we talked awhile, went to breakfast, and started arranging our room. My parents did buy me a small television to put in the room. It only came in black and white, color TV was still very expensive to have in 1979.

(Nobody is perfect.)

During our first week, I learned a little too much about my new friend. He had people coming into our room all during the day and evening. I could not study because all the interruptions. The nights that I did not have early classes, we would go to the running track and jog one or two miles. Ironically, when we were through, we would go to the bottom of a hill and race to the top. The loser had to buy the first pitcher of beer at the club, But, again, we would get back to our room, he would have friends that would come in and smoke some pot.

Before the end of the week, I realized that he had other things than pot and I saw him do a sell. Then it hit me! (DUH) He was the college dealer. He was being so nice to me so that I would stay quiet. By that Friday, I told him it was too much for me to handle and try to study so I was going to ask for my own room. I promised him I would not tell anyone and he said that he still wanted to jog together, and that when I was drunk, he would let me come over and take a freebie use to not be hungover. I agreed.

(Giving up air condition)

When I asked to be moved, I said that my roommate had too many friends over nightly and I could not study. They agreed if I was willing to go to the dorm that did not have air conditioning. There were no places to put me in the air conditioned dorm. (It was cheaper) I had no choice so I accepted it. It was cooling down anyway, so I had nothing to really lose. For the record, I only smoked the bong less than ten times. I definitely liked having my own room, too.

(This is just the beginning of college. more to come in Blog 25}

Blog 25: Catching Up On Things, Then continue

(I can't wait to add new pictures!)

I hope everyone had a great Holiday season and a great start to 2018! I admit mine was not the best. I have been sick, had a bad time with the change to the new year, and lost a close cousin on New Year's Eve, I found out that I had cataracts in both eyes (which explains some of writing mistakes! LOL

I began my cataract surgeries yesterday. The right eye was the worst so we started with it. It will be February by the time I get both eyes finished. So, for the readers, I will probably be doing shorter, but more blogs! As for my cousin dying, I am both glad and sad! She had a long bout with cancer, her hurting but not complaining. She was my medical supporter and I was hers. For the last few years we kept each other uplifted and assured someone was praying for each of us.

Her memorial was this past Saturday, and I was asked to lead the music and, also, sing a solo. It was quite an honor and I luckily knew the songs. (Since I could not see the words!) I felt good and I feel I did the song justice, even though it was acapella! At least people were saying I stayed in key. The song was "You Raise Me Up" including the second verse. I will miss you greatly, cuz, and thank you for your comfort.

Blog 26: Finalizing my short college life

("I am here for you unconditionally, as long as you feed me!!!)

(How could this happen!! I was an A student!!)

   As I planned my first semester of college, I was was basing it on pre-med necessities mixed with Freshmen requirements. (18 credit hours) I was given a rude awakening to realize what little I really knew. My Calculus 1 class was the worst. The professor went through everything I knew within the first 3 classes. I then realized, "You know what? I am really going to have to study!!!!" My English class was divided into two parts. Learning the reason for proper English and comparing different beliefs in how we should live. The second part was composition. I had to write three compositions using notes, having to document my resources, and one about your life, in general.

   My Biology class was my favorite and it involved a lab with it for 1 credit hour. It was my first class and I thought I would be smart and buy a recorder to use so I could review it again later. Of course, things were not going to go the way I planned. This was a large class and was held in an auditorium. I sat about midway up and sat with my new friends. The Professor began and I turned on my recorder. Immediately, this loud screeching noise was rebounding through the classroom. In reaching for it, I pushed the recorder to the floor and started scrambling to turn it off. People were laughing and you can guess my embarrassment. The professor kindly said he was flattered but he did not think I would need the recorder. WELCOME TO COLLEGE!

(Beginning the party life)

Even though I had what was considered a "tough" schedule, I found myself having a lot of free time. I was welcomed into a group of partiers and it was never a day that I did not have at least a beer. If nothing was happening at the school, I tried to come home every other week. (Remember, for me to be in choir, I had to attend Mass and sing in their choir every other Sunday.)

One such Sunday, we sang at the reopening of a cathedral. The priest was given a new pocket watch, a certificate, and the first six months of payments. Everyone was yelling, "Speech! Speech!" After the applaud died down, he said, "All I want to say is that it took 47 days, 105 man hours, and about 120 CASES of beer to complete this job!" My mouth had dropped to the floor. Did he really say that? (He was given a standing ovation!) This was a severe shock to li'l ol' country baptist boy, me!

On these weekends, I hung around my college friends and I would sometimes date this beautiful Hispanic girl. I was not a full gentleman, but I could not go all the way with her. Goodness knows I tried! However, I would stop myself right before the act. One day, in front of a few friends, she asked me if I were gay. I denied it and told her I respected her too much. That was our last date.

I began dating one of her friends who I really was not interested in. I found that, after partying, I could go all the way with her. Also, when

I would come home, I would party with my old friends, which when I would go home dateless, I knew that I could go to certain bars and be picked up within a half hour. It did not happen that way every time I went home, I did get lucky with a girl, every now and then.

Cont....in **blog 27......**

Blog 27: Finishing College and Partying for awhile, joining the Navy

(Get back, girl!, I saw him first!!!)

(Leaving St Edwards in Austin, moving to Colorado for my second semester and its debacle, making up my freshmen year in the summer and more)

I need to apologize about leaving my last blog in talking about my sex life. But, the rest of this series changes and I wanted to start this Blog at its beginning. My grades made me want to get serious about studies, as well. I made my FIRST C ever. It was devastating. Since my scholarship ended, I moved up to Colorado early enough to claim residency so I could go to Colorado State in Boulder. I could live with my Sister and Brother-in-Law to save money and stay away from the party people. And I began going back to church.

My classes were to finish the second semester of what I took in Austin. Biology 2 with lab, Computer Math, English 2, swimming. (12 credit hours) My classes were spread out very weirdly. I had Biology lab every Monday morning. Computer math, English 2 were on Tuesday and Thursday. Swimming was Every Wednesday and Friday in the morning. Finally, Biology was a 3 hour night class on Wednesday. This made a long day on Wednesday and only Swimming on Friday.

In my second week, I realized that I was doing the same work in Biology and English as I did in Austin. I showed the counselors and they dropped me and I lost an entire semester. So, I became a lead manager at a Jack-in the Box to make money because I met a beautiful green eyed, redhead at church. She was 17 and I was 18, turning 19. My Brother-in-Law and sister were the leaders of the youth group at their church. My first weekend in Colorado, the youth were going up in the mountains to snow tube. I went, also.

I talked to this girl all through dinner, Friday night. I definitely was not prepared to sleep in the cold, so I tried to stay up all night in the main room with a few of the youth, including this girl. I did not have enough energy to stay awake, and I fell asleep. I started freezing. By morning, though, I was very warm. I awoke to having my head in her lap and about 6 blankets covering me. She had stayed up all night making sure I was comfortable and warm. It was love at first night!

By late spring, I was offered a medical job as an allergy technologist back in Dallas making twice the money and I could go to Eastfield Community College in the summer and catch my credits back up. I gave the girl a promise ring for when she graduated. But, like most long distance relationships, she sent back my ring. The bad news was that, feeling rejected again, I got plastered and went where I knew I would be accepted. The good news was that I took four summer classes and got all A's. This ended my freshmen year with an A- total. What was funny was that Vanessa ended up in two of my classes unplanned. (Economics 1 & 2)

My job and getting my brother, Darrell, to be my roommate, enabled me to move into an apartment. I had money to party with Steve and my other friends a lot. Our new hangout was the Don Carter's All-night bowling center off of Central Expressway. What trouble we got ourselves into when we were there? However, I felt my life going backwards, so my next step was to join the Navy to finish school, (and get paid while I did it.) This will begin Blog 29.

Blog 28: Finalizing my civilian and joining the Navy

(The sailor suit that my nephew is wearing was passed down to each of my nephews born after him. I have a picture of each one of them wearing it, thanks to my sister-in-law, Les.)

(What led me to join the Navy. saying goodbye to Anthony after our years of bonding)

To finish off the first third of my life and the beginning of my Navy Years, I must explain the final blow of my party year. When I came home from Colorado, I got in late. Anthony was already asleep, but Anna placed him on my bed because he was crying that he was going to miss me coming home. I went in my room, shook him a little, and he smiled and gave me the biggest hug and kiss on the cheek. He said he loved me and I said it back. He waited for me to get in bed and he put his arms around my neck then fell asleep again. It was the closest thing to feeling like a father that I have ever had.

The next year and a half, I did try to spend time with him. Anna had remarried and it did not last long, but she got pregnant again and had my niece, Shelley. She moved out of my parents house about the same time Darrell and I moved to our apartment. She met my brother-in-law (David) and they got married within the year. When they did, Anna announced that they were moving to Midland, Texas so they could become a true family and get a new start.

My heart broke, even though I was very happy for her. The day they left, I felt my entire being was vacated. I had nothing to look forward to happening, because I partied too much. When I realized that I would never go back to college, and had no place to grow inside the allergy clinic, I started looking at other offers. A friend, who had joined the Navy already, gave me the idea to join, too. He said I could go to the Naval school and they would pay FOR my college, as well as, be PAID while going. I simply would sign up for 6 years active duty to pay them back.

By February, 1981, I decided this was my only way out. I began going through the early sign up things, such as testing, medical physicals, and personal conversations with my recruiter. In the sign up forms (at that time), they had a question that asked if I were homosexual. Since I still wanted to get married and have kids, and I did have hetero-relationships. I truthfully felt I could answer "no". And truthfully, I did not look forward to spending 10 weeks with all guys. I made a pact with God to get me through boot camp.

My enlistment date was set for April 13, 1981. Boot camp was going to be in Florida, also, this was the boot camp for all female enlistees. I finally had to go to my parents and tell them what I was planning to do. I waited until my Birthday, March 29th, so that they would not have enough time to try and change my mind. My dad was livid and my mom was scared. They chose to take me to the recruiting station and as I got out of the car, my dad pleaded for me to change my mind. I simply reminded him that he did not care enough to help me pay for college and it left me no choice. I kissed them good-bye and I went inside.

This is where I will leave volume one. In volume two, I will tell about my life in the Navy and help explain that though I did not know at the time, God still had plans for me and I needed to open my eyes!

Printed in the United States
by Baker & Taylor Publisher Services